AUDACIOUS ARCHITECTURE

AUDACIOUS ARCHITECTURE

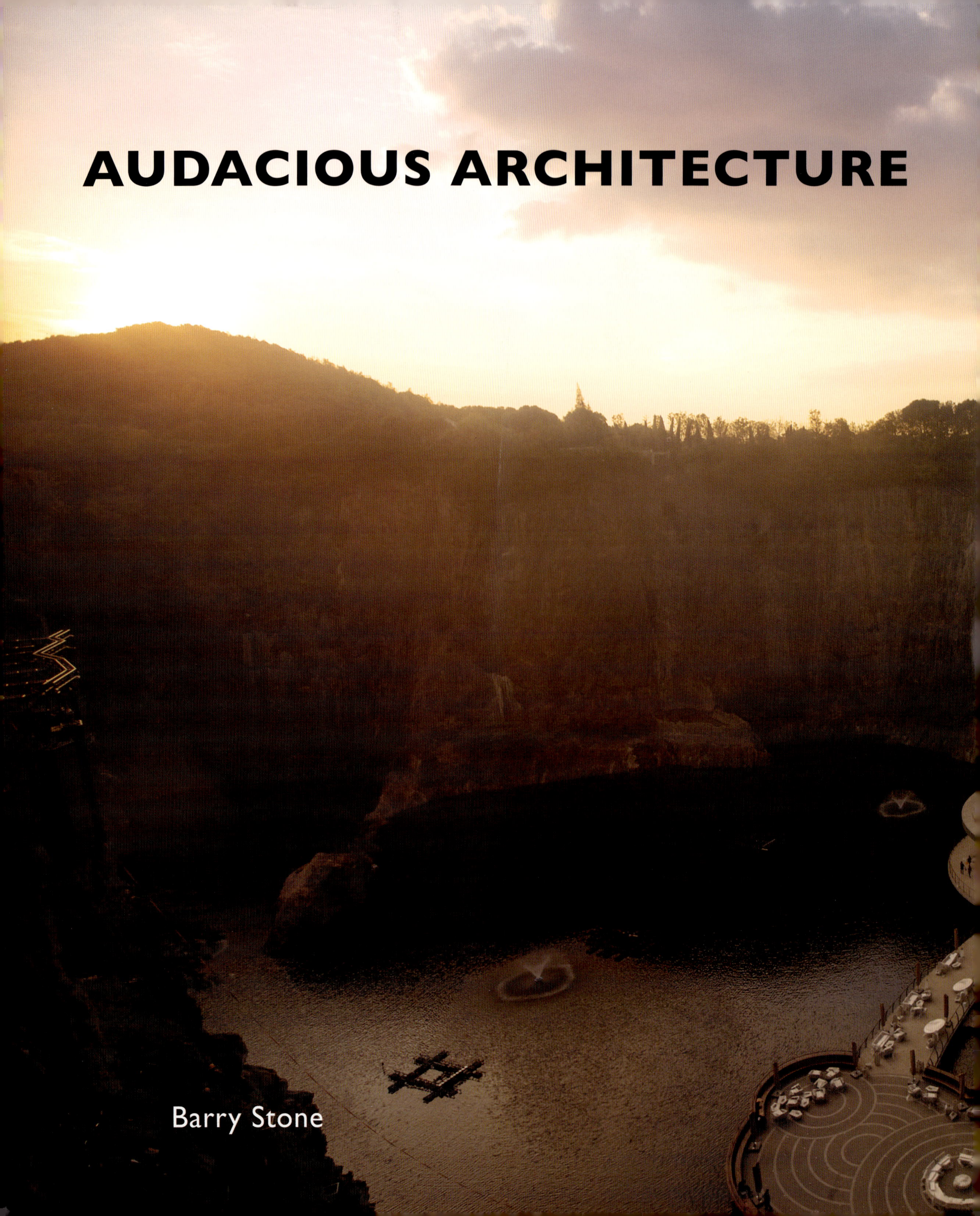

Barry Stone

NEW HOLLAND

CONTENTS

“All fine architectural values are human values, else not valuable.”

FRANK LLOYD WRIGHT, ARCHITECT, 1908

INTRODUCTION

The only treatise on the subject of western architecture to have survived Antiquity is a series of ten books titled *De Arquitectura, or Ten Books on Architecture, written in the 1st Century BCE by* Marcus Vitruvius, a Roman military engineer and architect who believed a building's integrity rested upon three fundamental principles: *utilitas* (functionality), *firmitas* (strength), and *venustas* (beauty). Vitruvius believed buildings should reflect the 'architecture of the body', and that buildings and humans, when at their most beautiful, shared one over-riding principal: symmetry.

Vitruvius thought a building was made beautiful through symmetry, by the mirroring of components across a vertical or horizontal central line, or axis. Symmetry, in Vitruvius' time, not only helped bring structures together, to raise them into a unified whole it also reflected a sense of logic and order, two aesthetics long held dear by the Ancient Romans and before them, the Greeks for whom the absence of proportion and symmetry meant only one thing. Chaos.

By the 6th century mathematics had become a kind of shorthand that allowed for the inclusion of symmetry into the ratios and geometric forms of buildings to define their spatial form. Mathematics, geometry, science – these disciplines were always the drivers behind the things we've built. In the 1400s the Italian designer Filippo Brunelleschi discovered the principles of linear perspective, the illusion of depth drawn on a flat surface, and immediately applied it to architecture. In the late 1700s the French mathematician Gaspard Monge invented descriptive geometry, the representation on two dimensions of a real or imaginary three dimensional object – such as a building.

In the 17th century Claude Perrault, the French architect best remembered for his role in the design and creation of the east façade of the Louvre Museum in Paris, wrote that what is or is not thought beautiful should be decided not by academics but by the person on the street. Perrault, the man who ironically was responsible for the translation of Vitruvian's *Ten Books on Architecture* into French, asserted that whether a building was beautiful or not was no longer dependent upon outdated notions of form that were restrictive and led to the creation of a lot of buildings many of which looked like the

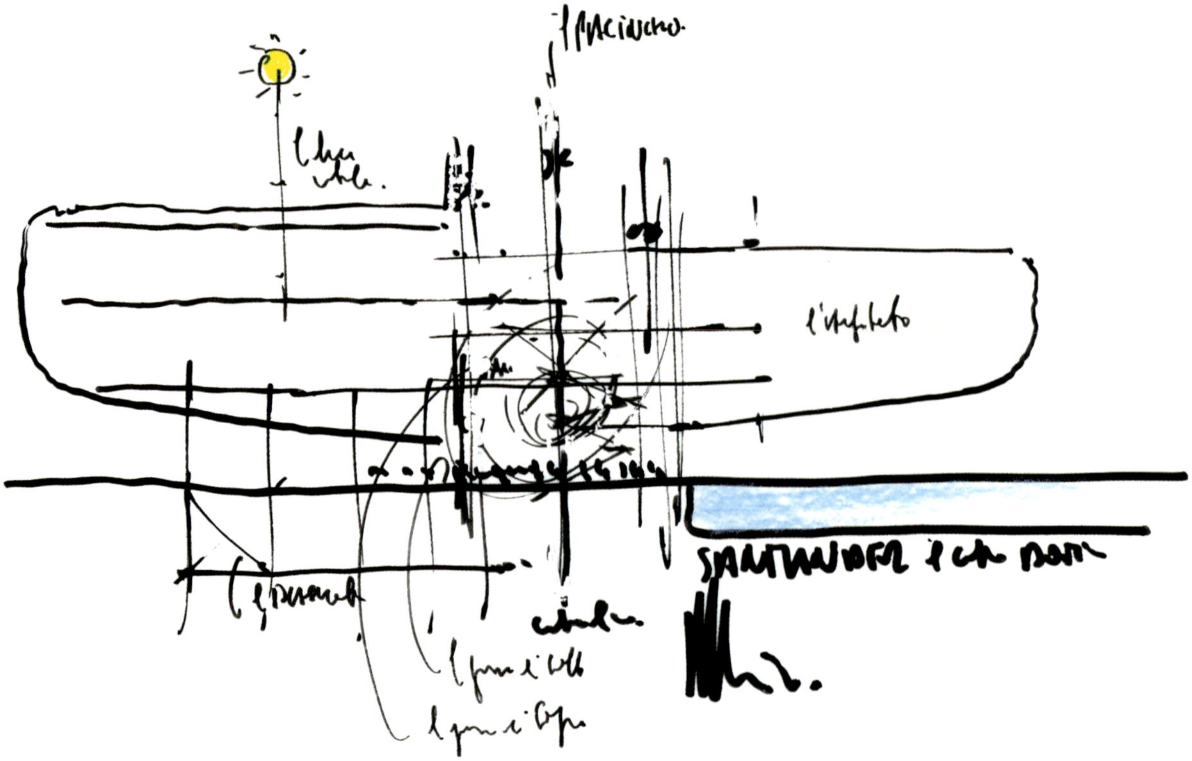

mirror image of each other. A building's worth, he said, should now rest in the eye of the beholder . . . and its designer. For its time, it was a monumental statement.

In the early 20th century modern architects began to turn to the rectilinear geometry of the Greek mathematician Euclid in the creation of a new era of buildings that emphasized the horizontal and the vertical, with balconies, walls and roof planes that intersected each other. The Rietveld Schröder House, designed in Utrecht in The Netherlands in 1924 by the Dutch furniture designer Gerrit Rietveld was a radical departure from everything that came before it, its upper level an open area that could be subdivided using a system of revolving and sliding panels. A glimpse of things to come.

In the 21st century symmetry still has a role to play, but it's only one element in a broad palette of creative options that architects now have at their disposal. Given free reign to bring their visions to life, architects now have a capacity for inventiveness that was once the preserve of painters. The world that had once been the domain of Dali, Klee, Miro, Chagall and Picasso – a realm of cubism, impressionism, surrealism and more – was now available in concrete, glass and steel to the likes of Koolhaas, Hadid, and Gehry.

Architecture has always been driven by innovation. The inherent inflexibility of concrete has led to the development of polymer microfibres, added to create a material 50 times as strong as traditional concrete but much lighter and able to flex under pressure. Low-cost smart windows can vary the amount of light that enters a room. Timber, the construction industry's oldest ally, is being panelized and cross-laminated, a process that imbues it with incredible strength and a surprising degree of fire resistance. Tall wooden buildings are once again beginning to appear anew in cityscapes around the world, causing some to ask whether timber might again become the future of urban construction.

But nowhere has the revolution in architecture we see now owed more to innovation than in the world of computer software. In the late 20th century CAD – Computer-Aided Design – came of age. Suddenly manual drafting, the art of creating drawings

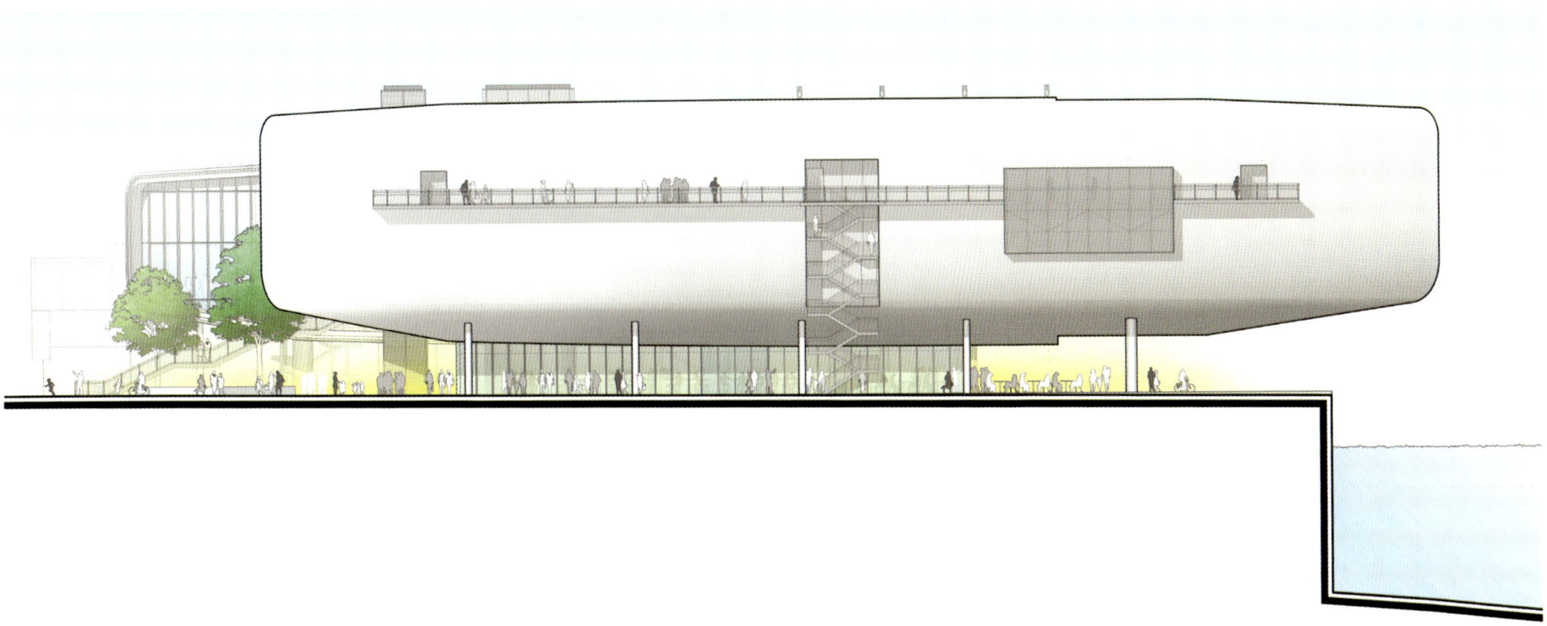

using pen and paper, was in danger of becoming obsolete. Computer assisted drafting has altered our approach to architecture every bit as much as the invention of the truss, the introduction of Roman concrete (*opus caementicium*), flying buttresses and the brick kiln.

The CAD revolution is now considered by designers the world over to represent the single greatest advance in construction history, enabling the creation of a whole new generation of complex geometric structures and testing them in a virtual world prior to breaking ground, designs once impossible to realize from drafts or cardboard models.

Suddenly hundreds of engineers and designers could be brought together from around the world to create a new array of designs and perspectives. Mathematical formulas were being created within the spreadsheet design. Wind tunnel tests using CAD technology, for instance, were used to test the impact of wind on the Burj Khalifa in Dubai, the world's tallest building.

Advances in software and the refining of new materials, such as perforated polymer concrete panels, translucent wood and pollution-absorbing bricks, coupled with the ability to calculate load-bearing stresses means anything is possible. A piece of artfully crumpled paper, a hurried sketch on a restaurant napkin – the first thoughts of an architect are no longer necessarily only an abstract concept from which something more orthodox will come.

The abstract concept can now itself be realized.

Good architecture should be a rejection of mediocrity. The Polish-American architect Daniel Libeskind, whose Museum of Zhang Zhidong appears in this book, described architecture as a kind of poetry, a poetic pursuit, and that without this poetic element architecture would devolve into something bordering on the needless. All of the architects whose work appears in this book believe buildings can change the world – one street at a time – and that by making positive change, by creating beautiful spaces, buildings have the capacity to make people happy.

It is hoped the buildings in this book will provide a glimpse forward to a better, happier world.

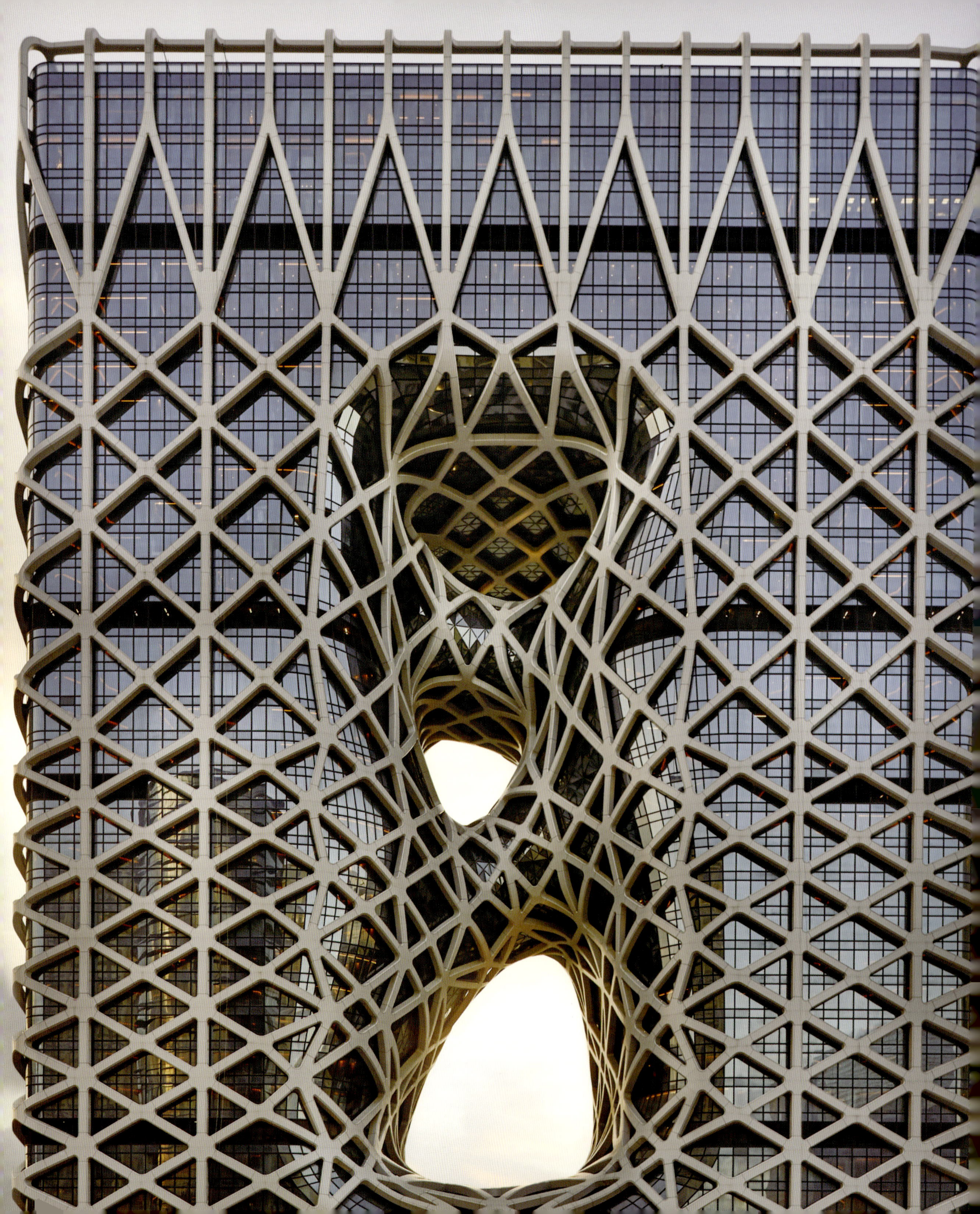

CHAPTER 1

Morpheus Hotel

Macau, China

Zaha Hadid Architects

In architecture a building's structural elements – its columns, walls etc – are neither designed to be, nor are they meant to be, aesthetically pleasing. They exist to perform a function; they give a building its strength, its integrity, its rigidity. They stop it from falling down. Located out of sight in the structure's interior, their presence also allows for the building's façade, now relieved of any meddlesome load-bearing duties, to be made beautiful with endless variations of glazed exteriors and fanciful ornamentation. The façade becomes the building's makeup, its face to the world. But what if things were reversed? What if internal structural elements were placed not in a building's interior, where they are rarely seen and almost without exception grossly underappreciated, but on the outside for all to see? What if all the hidden engineering that allowed a structure to exist at all, became its façade? And not just functional – designed to be beautiful? And what impact would this radical inversion have upon its internal design, now that it is freed of all the annoying barriers it would otherwise have to avoid?

Welcome to the world of the architectural exoskeleton.

Buildings with exoskeletons, such as the NEO Bankside residential development in London and the decades-old but still striking HSBC Headquarters in Hong Kong, will never lose their allure. Their confidence, their bravado, are laid bare. They bring engineering out of the shadows. And few buildings on the planet have transformed the discipline of engineering and given it the celebrity status it deserves more than the Morpheus Hotel on the island of Macau, the masterpiece of Zaha Hadid Architects.

Built over the abandoned foundations of a condominium project that was never realized, the hotel was unveiled in June 2018 and set back from Macau's main Cotai Strip, lost little time in becoming one of the world's most identifiable buildings. Resembling a double helix the world's first free-form exoskeleton high-rise is immediately recognisable thanks to its unique geometric façade punctuated by three astonishing holes. Lauded for pioneering new approaches in the design of steel and aluminium exoskeletons, it is a sculptural triumph of form and function, a new kind of building designed as a singular extrusion emerging from the extant, abandoned foundations below. What began as a traditional rectangular footprint quickly morphed into a 40 story building with two internal circulation cores set within a twisting monolithic volume that was able to have its freed-up interior 'carved out' into a series of sumptuous voids. These voids provided plenty of space to work with, space that would enable it to easily stay under the 525 foot high development envelope demanded by local planners.

The British-based engineering consultancy BuroHappold Engineering were appointed to oversee the exoskeleton's design and construction, and would not have been able to do so without using Finite Element (FEM) analysis, a program that employs algebraic equations to solve complex engineering problems. Working to a tight 12 month timeframe BuroHappold employees had to create an array of bespoke computer programs just to help make sense of the daunting number of FEM models that were required to create the building's vine-like exterior.

Behind the scenes, of course – out of sight in walls and floors and tucked away in high ceilings – there is much that deserves mention. Temperature sensors control the underfloor heating in the guest bathrooms. Heat gain in hotel rooms is diminished with the use of ½ inch thick glass, double glazed with a 2/3 inch gap. Some windows, depending on their orientation were treated with polyvinyl to prevent noise penetration. Fresh air is regulated with the help of air delivery units based on the 3rd, 19th and 39th

floors, with stale air allowed to rise up before being expelled from the building through its upper levels. Heating coils help maintain comfortable temperatures in the lobby and throughout the central atrium. And because Macau is in a typhoon-prone region the building had to be able to withstand not only punishing winds, but also massive volumes of rainwater. So modeling resulted in the design of a unique rainwater system capable of dispersing in excess of 8½ inches of rainfall every hour.

Yet despite all of the impressive technical innovations here that you cannot see, it's what you see on that mesmerising exterior that will always stubbornly steal the limelight. There are in excess of thirty façade profiles. There's faceted glazing, single-curved glazing, flat glazing and triangulated free-form glazing. The complicated geometry meant it wouldn't be possible to design the hotel using traditional two dimensional drawings, so the Rhino 3D CAD application, coupled with a visual programming language known as Grasshopper was used. Exoskeleton nodes needed to align with floor beams; stud beams needed to be both perpendicular and horizontal to the façade's face. But it wasn't all high tech. A wire frame model was used to help determine which program could best be used to determine the deployment of the building's glazed surfaces, each piece of which was unique to its location.

The flagship hotel of the City of Dreams Resort complex, Morpheus Hotel is two distinct towers connected by a series of floating passageways. Its cavernous central atrium links its north and south-facing façades, while bridges between each of the voids connect its public spaces and are home to restaurants, bars and lounges. Twelve glass elevators provide vertigo-inducing internal views, and its three horizontal vortices provide external views from the majority of its 770 rooms. The rooftop swimming pool, surrounded by the same sinuous, skeletal forms seen on its façade, has the look and feel of some hidden, secret place.

Rooms, restaurants, swimming pools. Normally this is the stuff of a hotel, the sort of things we all think matter. How refreshing, then, to find a hotel where the usual things can't compete with the building itself. Sure, its rooms are designed by Peter Remedios, one of the world's most gifted hotel designers, and two of its four restaurants' menus are prepared in collaboration with that icon of French cooking, Alain Ducasse. But inspired interior design and mouth-watering food are hardly uncommon ingredients in 5-star hotels these days. What really matters are the less familiar things, things like Rhino, FEM and Grasshopper, radius edges and horizontal vortices, heterogeneous loops and faceted windows, isometrics and orthogonal grids.

How ironic it all is: a building in which style has become substance; and substance, style.

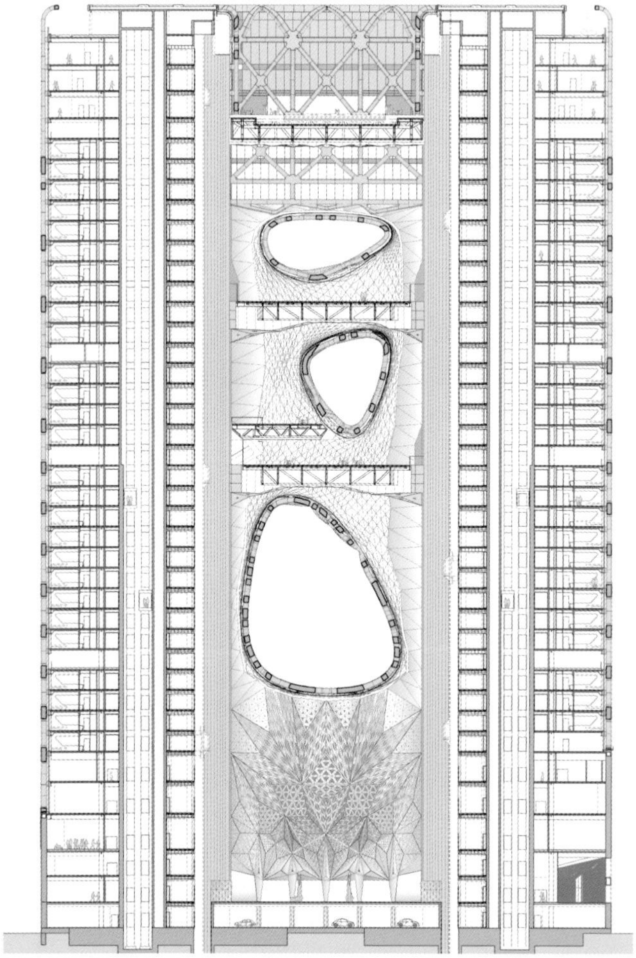

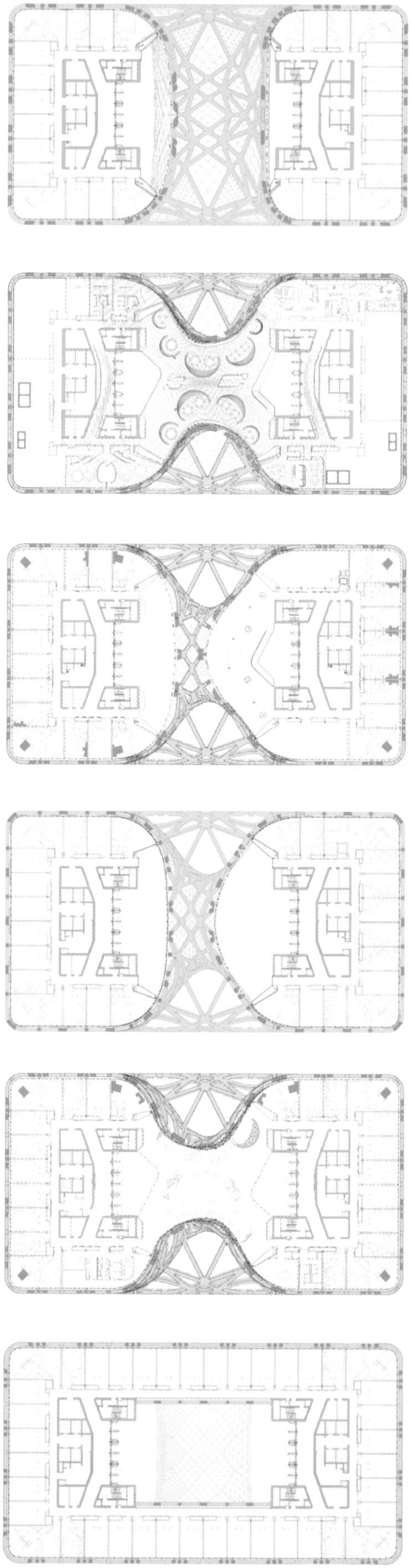

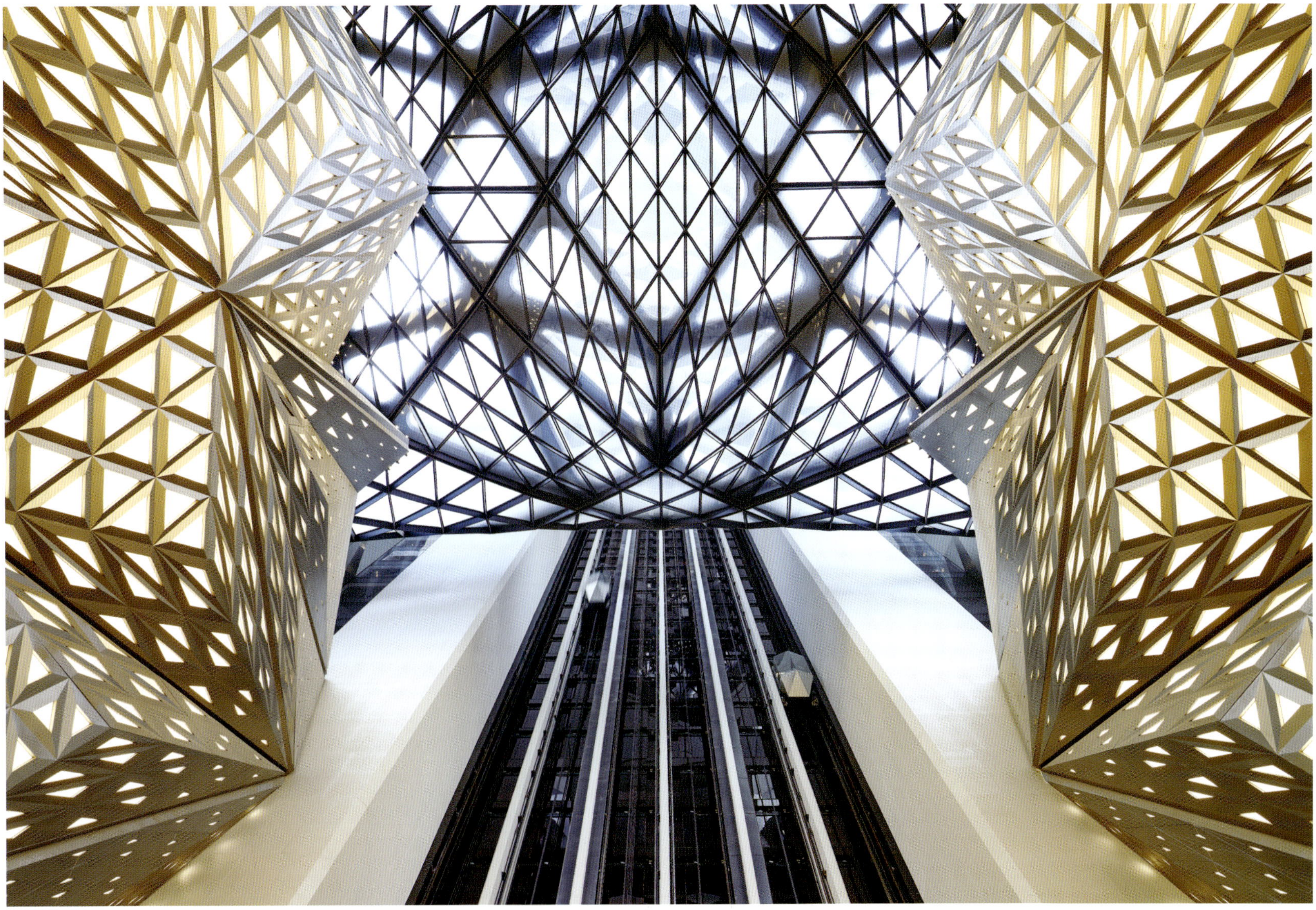

CHAPTER 2

Amangiri

Kane County, Utah, USA

Wendell Burnette, Marwan Al-Sayed, Rick Joy & Michael Boucher

Amangiri Resort is nestled in Canyon Point in southern Utah, hidden from view within a 600 acre, 180-million-year-old natural sanctuary of hoodoos, escarpments, caves and mesas; a world of ancient sand dunes frozen in time, defined and shaped by wind and water.

It began as the simplest of ideas and the most basic of forms when one of Amangiri's principal architects, Wendell Burnette, unwrapped a block of cast earth in front of the legendary hotelier Adrian Zecha, creator of the Aman group of properties. Zecha had found the ideal site for his new hotel: a mile-high plateau surrounded by cryptobiotic soils and over a dozen species of sage, in a canyon where the desert light changes by the minute during the day, and by night sits like some endless montage of van Gogh's *Starry Night*.

Completed in 2009, Amangiri is a triumph of monolithic volumes and geometric purity, a kaleidoscope of concrete defined by straight lines, squares, rectangles, mesmerising vanishing points and a mix of angular planes immersed in a world of eroded sandstone where man-made volumes just don't belong.

… or do they? After all, here is a building that defies its man-made nature. The natural sands and aggregates that give it its shape were sourced within a 100 mile radius of the site (17 percent of which is waste fly ash from a nearby Navajo power station). The silica – a natural ingredient in sandstone and itself compressed over eons of geologic time – was also sourced locally. Utilising 5 ft x 12 ft panels of Finn-Form the concrete was mixed on site and imbued with a phenolic resin to give it its tactile, glass-like smoothness. Bob Kirk, the great architect/concrete guru was asked to join the process and selected the inert oxide pigments that would provide Amangiri's concrete its empathic relationship to the surrounding entrada sandstone.

Rarely has concrete ever been used with such affection. Breezeways funnel and then cool warm desert winds, skylights reminiscent of local Navajo hogans provide conduits of light onto windowless spaces, while narrowing pathways frame vivid perspectives onto distant escarpments.

In the same way as the paintings of the Dutch artist Piet Mondrian showed that paint could exist simply as lines and shapes free of representation, Amangiri seems almost oblivious to its role, refusing to allow any notions of what a hotel 'should' be to interfere with its audacious form. In the same way Frank Gehry's Guggenheim Museum in Bilbao, Spain has become more feted than the art it was built to enclose, the creation of architects Wendell Burnette, Marwan Al-Sayed, Rick Joy and landscape architect Michael Boucher has achieved far greater significance than merely the provision of meals and shelter.

It's as though it doesn't even care it's a hotel.

Nevertheless, it *is* a hotel, with 34 Mesa and Desert View suites all accessed via private courtyards; their beds raised on cement platforms overlooking terraces each with their own fire pit; their flat roofs with beds. The 3,745 square ft Amangiri Suite comes with an 60 ft swimming pool with floating steps, a sky view terrace and private sun deck, while the 25,000 sq ft spa contains five treatment rooms and uses traditional Navajo healing techniques to restore a sense of *hozho* – the pursuit of beauty, balance and harmony.

At Amangiri's heart is the swimming pool. Heated to a tropical 86 degrees Fahrenheit it curls around the resort's most defining natural feature, a rounded boulder of Entrada sandstone that descends into the pool from the escarpment above and is the absolute last word in desert aesthetics. Amangiri was sited where it is because of it, the pool was designed to affectionately hug it, and the resort in turn hugs the pool. Like a wagon train drawing itself into a circle in the Old West.

Step over your terrace into the desert and you can hike a network of on-property trails, ride a horse, or climb one or all four of the resort's Via Ferratas (Italian for Iron Road) – climbing routes established by the resort's onsite guides that includes the Hoodoo ascent – 490 feet straight up the side of Studhorse Mesa using ropes and climbing anchors. There's also a steel 240 foot-long suspension bridge over a 426 foot-high chasm. At Amangiri, you can feel as comfortable or as challenged as you like.

The food is prepared in an energetic, open kitchen that showcases regional Native American cuisine as well as lobsters from Maine, barramundi from Japan and prawns from the Sea of Cortez. Amangiri chefs also visit surrounding Native American

communities to collect a range of soon-to-be recognized 'super foods' such as cholla cactus buds, the needles of which are extracted individually by Navajo women so the buds can be used in soups, casseroles, even antipasto salads.

But beyond the rooms; beyond the food and the trails and even, perhaps, the architecture, there remains the sheer longevity that is represented by Amangiri's unrelenting volumes of concrete – the one essential material that was imagined from the beginning, providing an immovable footprint that will span the ages. Only concrete can be at home with the timeless landscapes here, can stand shoulder to shoulder with it and go the distance into eternity.

Imagining what things Amangiri might witness over what will be a considerable lifetime so intrigued me that I rang architect Wendell Burnette at his offices in Phoenix, Arizona to ask him if he thought he'd accidentally created some kind of 'pre-ruin' ediface, something that is so permanent that it is destined to deteriorate, to decay. And he laughed.

'We actually conceived of it as resembling a kind of ruin. We wondered how one might transform an existing ruin in the future, how might you re-inhabit it, or re-define it. I mean . . . almost certainly now, in the 21st century, you'd fill it with plumbing and wiring. But then what? What does it become? In this case, well, we were asked to create a hotel.

'... and so we did'.

CHAPTER 3

Foro Boca

Boca del Río, Mexico

Rojkind Arquitectos

What's not to like about board-formed concrete? The process of patterning concrete in such a way as to create a wood-grained, board-like image, a textured, three-dimensional imprint to an otherwise cool, flat surface is becoming an increasingly popular element in modern design – and is rarely seen put to better effect than in the exterior surfaces of the Foro Boca ('Forum at the Mouth') Concert Hall at the mouth of the Jamapa River in Boca del Río, in the Mexican state of Veracruz.

This triumphant building, now home to the Boca del Río Philharmonic Orchestra, is reminiscent of neolithic examples of 'monumental' architecture, the carving of structures from a single piece of rock, or the cutting and placement of multiple large stones. Looking like a series of sculptured, uplifted tectonic plates, the spirit of monumentalism seems alive and well on the Boca del Río waterfront. Foro Boca – which began conceptually as a single large box deconstructed into smaller volumes to provide it with scale when seen from the pier, beach and city – now rises up, its concrete exterior of gorgeously anchored floating volumes and angular walls exhibiting a rare degree of geometric purity, made all the more aesthetic – if not downright mesmerising – by the diagonal patterns of those 'wooden' concrete boards.

Foro Boca mountainous, a cluster of cubed volumes as jagged and block-like as the concrete blocks that line the town's coastal defences, its textured surface designed to develop a patina that will, in time, compliment the rocks along the nearby breakwater. At first glance it seems as though the building has no front or back, its entrance being hidden underneath a magnificent 7.5 foot-high cantilevered volume, which provides protection against the site's strong north winds at the same time it threatens to compress you with its sheer bulk. Once you pass under it and into the foyer, however, the building opens up into an internal, light-filled void: a three-story atrium punctuated by carefully placed apertures that funnel and filter light down into the building's cave-like heart.

Once inside, three elements dominate: granite, concrete . . . and wood. A network of animated, slatted wooden walkways crisscross the interior, leading to various access points, while a welcoming lack of ornamentation concentrates your eyes on the *form* of

the place, reminding you that here is a building so chock-full of confidence, so assured and pure in its design and purpose that to add anything would border on the negligent. You'll find no distractions here.

Inside there is a 966-seat auditorium that can be adapted for theatrical and dance performances, a 150-seat rehearsal room, and a mix of flexible spaces including a musical library. Outside, the creation of a new public plaza provides ample space from which to admire the building's many facets. A granite boulevard was laid, the existing breakwater was transformed into a pedestrian walkway with a fabulous angular guardrail, and expansive new terraces provide views over the Gulf of Mexico. And thanks to Foro Boca's wealth of flat internal and external façades it can easily be transformed into an impromptu textured concrete cinema screen for the showing of films, documentaries and other audio-visual presentations.

Michel Rojkind, the founder of Rojkind Arquitectos, told *Architizer* he feels the building succeeds as a transitional structure between the breakwater and the city. 'There's a fluidness to the way people move around the hall . . . it reflects the musical notes, it reflects the waves, it reflects the sound of the wind' which gives it a coherency. Rather than just working as a building, it 'cares' about the community it was built to serve.

The Boca del Río Philharmonic Orchestra was formed in 2014, and Foro Boca is the orchestra's first permanent home. Among its various philanthropic pursuits, the orchestra provides choral and orchestral tuition to the city's low-income children. The building is also able to host multiple events at the same time, including cultural programs designed to help the people of Boca del Río reach out to one another and to those beyond. Foro Boca has facilitated this outreach, bringing to fruition a long-realized dream of urban and social renewal in a once derelict precinct. Michel Rojkind also believes it will act as a lightning rod for further expressions of modernism that will continue to bring new life to this once neglected neighborhood at the mouth of Boca del Río's Jamapa River, proving once again that architecture is always at its best when it engages with, and inspires, the communities that surround it.

PUERTA 1
SALA MESTER

CHAPTER 4

Qatar National Library

Doha, Qatar

Rem Koolhaas / OMA

Located in Doha's Education City, an academic hub home to satellite campuses belonging to some of the world's leading universities and academic institutions, the Qatar National Library (QNL) is a monument to knowledge and a steward of Qatar's heritage. Within its 485,000 square feet you can find more than a million books displayed on shelves that rise up on a series of stepped tiers from the library's centre, providing an amphitheater-like appearance. The library also has more than 500,000 ebooks, as well as newspapers, periodicals, special collections in more than 20 languages (including early manuscripts and texts on Islamic and Arabic development) and photographs that trace the emergence of Qatar as a nation and that of the wider Gulf region. By any standard you care to use it is, first and foremost, a library: a monument to knowledge, tolerance, and dialogue.

The QNL has been designed to be a seamless amalgam of library and building. The bookshelves, the interior's single most important visual element, are far from the sort of 'necessary' items that are most library's *de rigueur*; not the sort you bring in off the back of a truck and just plonk down. These bookshelves are white marble – the same material as the floor – and include their own individual lighting and book return system … even their own ventilation. Because the bookshelves are not spread over a single, level space there is no sense of claustrophobia here, no feeling that books are somehow hidden, no endless aisles over the top of which you cannot see. Set in between and around the shelves and in the aisles are places where one can sit, read and socialize.

At the centre of the library, at its physical and metaphysical heart is the library's historic Heritage Collection, which includes a precious Ptolemaic map dating from 1478 and documents from the 7th Century BCE housed in a 19.5 foot-deep, vault-like space, a design that resembles many a Middle Eastern archaeological dig full of treasures and mysteries one can unearth and browse. The vault is clad in glorious beige travertine marble, giving it the stature and aura its collection of some of the Middle East's rarest manuscripts so richly deserves.

But beyond its repository of books, ebooks and manuscripts, it is the library as a *public meeting place* that the designers at OMA were equally interested in exploring. There are open spaces here for workshops, an auditorium for theatrical performances, and moveable screens in the main foyer than can be used to create impromptu, intimate spaces. The library's cavernous interior also dispels that staid notion that in libraries one needs to always speak in whispers. Here there is space enough to accommodate equally both books *and* talkative patrons in a building that does much to facilitate a *new* notion of what a library can be; not a place of silences that can create barriers to learning and limits the exchange of ideas, but rather a place that encourages gatherings, enquiry, friendship and discussion.

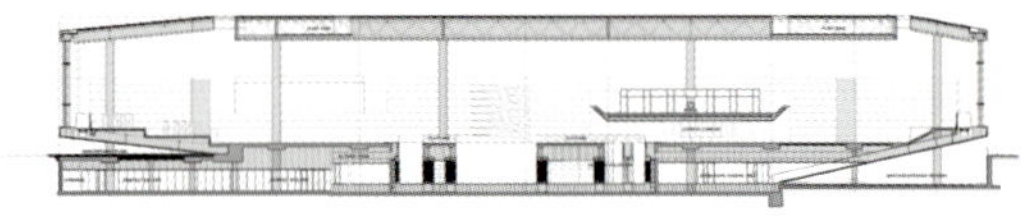

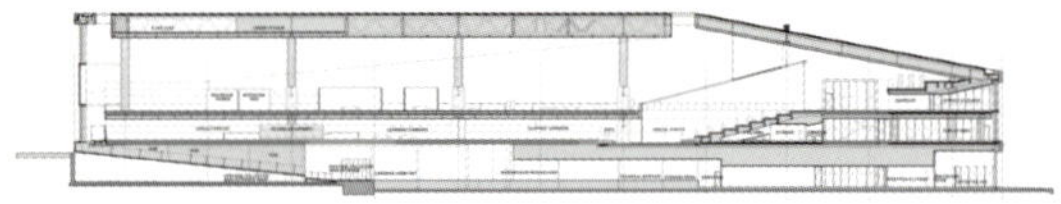

The library's books are arranged along three main aisles all of which are connected by a column-free bridge, itself a meeting place filled with study rooms, a conference table, multipurpose auditorium and reading tables all capable of being enclosed within one of the building's most striking elements: its Cosmic Curtain.

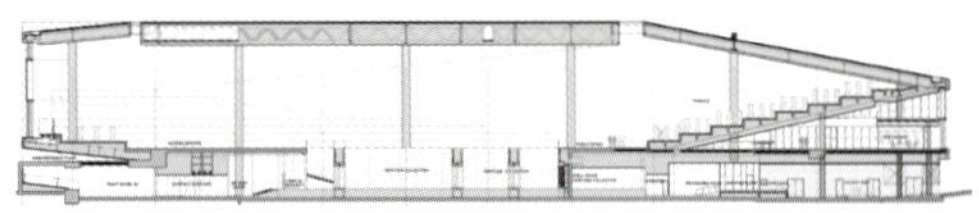

The curtain is the inspired creation of the Amsterdam-based design firm Inside Outside. Set on a specially designed track system its 7530 sq feet of fabric take the notion of 'curtain' to an entirely new level, turning it into one of the library's signature features. The curtain is a technical and aesthetic masterpiece, a loose weave of smooth and firm fibres held in place by a series of circles woven into the fabric. The fabric is light on the outside yet dark on the inside, its pattern of circles inspired by Qatar's night sky and the impressive collection of astrolabes housed in the nearby Museum of Islamic Art. Seventy-eight of the curtain's 96 panels feature a unique design. The curtain took Inside Outside two months of weaving to complete.

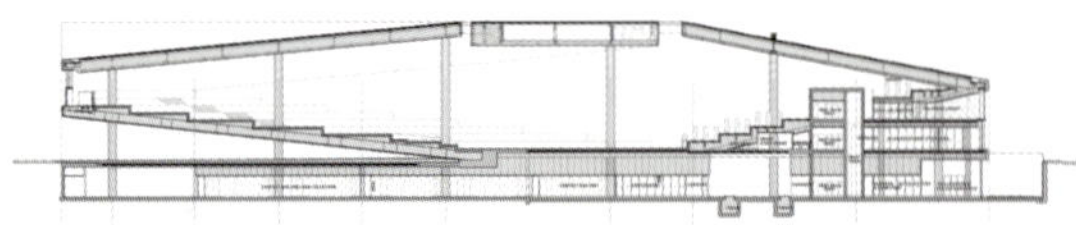

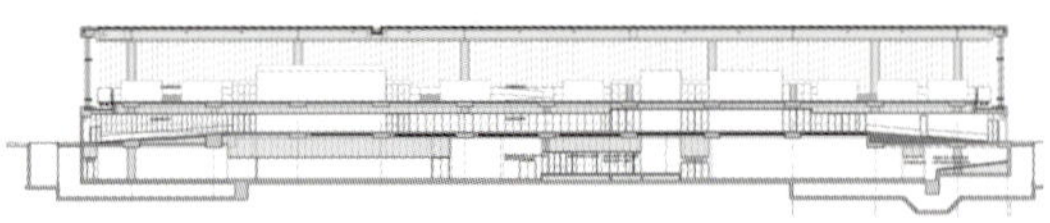

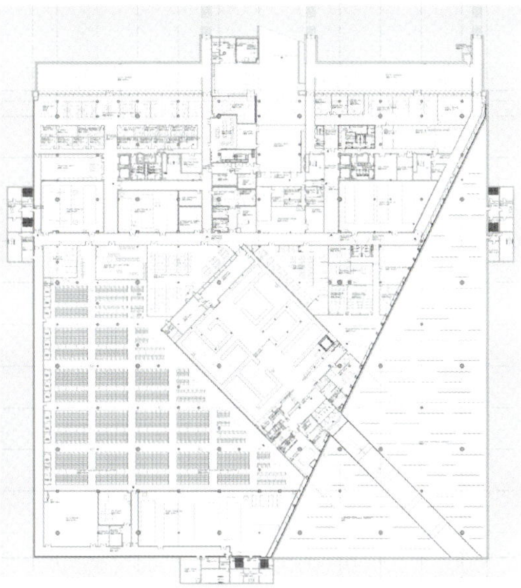

Inside Outside were also responsible for the library's external landscaping. The garden, a series of circular beds or 'imprints', each contain a family of drought-tolerant plants: Acacia, Agave and Euphorbia. Each planting is designed to be watered only in the first few years until they have established themselves, after which they will survive on their own and so provide educational experiment into how plants can independently survive Qatar's harsh, dry climate.

The Dutch architect and co-founder of OMA, Rem Koolhaas, grew up with a fascination for the 19th Century folk tales of the Brothers Grimm and spent endless hours as a young man in the Stedelijk Museum & Library in Amsterdam. Years later, in 1978, he all but appropriated a seat in the New York Public Library as he spent day and night scouring the library's considerable resources included microfilm, books and old newspapers. This was for the writing of *Delirious New York: A Retrospective Manifesto for Manhattan,* his ode to Manhattan as a prototype of the modern metropolis. 'With Manhattan as an example', he once wrote, 'this book is a blueprint for the culture of congestion'.

So when it came to finding an architect who would be best-placed to create a library of the 21st Century, an architect who could draw upon his own experience and understand firsthand the subtle inter-relationship between library and library user, one could hardly do better than enlist the services of this advocate of the energy of modernism, this life-long appreciator of the valued place the library has in society.

Koolhaas believes that libraries are ideal vehicles for the expression of radical architecture, and this is no exception. The 450 foot-long Qatar National Library building is a single open space, the same length as two 747's set end-to-end. There

would be no sense of separation here, no floors, no walls, just a single space with its striking diamond-shaped profile, all conceived as a single room, its edges raised off the ground so to provide a practical retreat from the ever-present Doha sun while at the same time providing the foundation for the tiered floor inside. The building's reduced footprint also gives it a small entry, which takes you up and into the library's heart where you emerge at the core of a veritable world of books that rise up around you.

A single room, indeed. Philip Johnson, the great American architect and winner of the very first Pritzker Architecture Prize in 1979, once said that the world's greatest buildings were all single rooms: Istanbul's Hafia Sofia and Blue Mosque, Chartres Cathedral outside Paris, and countless other Gothic masterpieces. The perfect realisation of a solitary chamber, he said, was the nearest an architect could ever hope to come to imitating the artistry of the painter's canvas. In the design and raising of QNL's overwhelming interior, OMA has done just that.

OMA's creation should also help dispel any qualms people might have of the demise of libraries in the digital age, thanks to an approach to design that reaffirms the importance and relevance of books through the use of technology. The rise of the ebook and the digitising of the written word is not seen here at QNL as some precursor to the book's demise, but rather as an invaluable tool in their ongoing preservation.

INTERCONTINENTAL

CHAPTER 5

Intercontinental Shanghai Wonderland

Shanghai, China

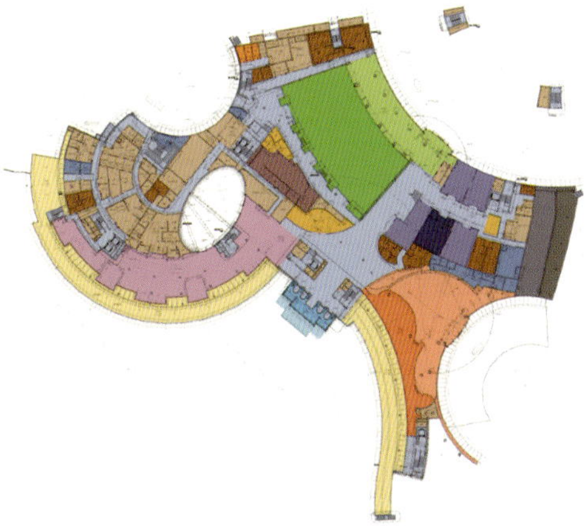

Martin Jochman with Studio Jade+QA (Concept with ATKINS)

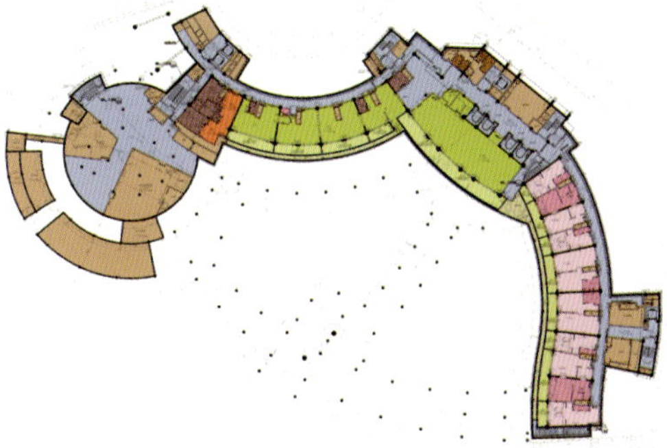

In 2013 in an abandoned quarry 18 miles outside Shanghai in the Sheshan Mountains, something extraordinary began to take shape. A structure with few parallels; a building in which 16 of its 18 floors were, in a sense, underground – or at least below the level of the surrounding ground. Yet it possessed expansive views of waterfalls and a unique, man-made lake. Rarely had an architect looked over a man-made scar upon the earth and seen such potential. And rarely has architecture taken by the throat such a hulking, tortured form and transformed it into a glittering prop for the building that now so triumphantly towers above it.

The Intercontinental Shanghai Wonderland is staggering in both its concept and scale: its 337 5-star rooms spread over 18 floors with views out over a World War II-era quarry that tightening environmental regulations forced to close in 2000; a once-dry pit now graced by purpose-built waterfalls. The hotel clings to a 295 foot-high cliff face, only two levels of it sited above the surrounding ground and which house the hotel's reception, restaurant and conference facilities. Its bulbous mid-section contains its sumptuous rooms – every one with its own balcony. Its two lower levels are located *underwater* and are home to another restaurant, additional rooms and an aquarium. The steel-framed monolith also has at its core a towering 'glass waterfall' that descends its entire length, a public space that is home to the hotel's observation lifts.

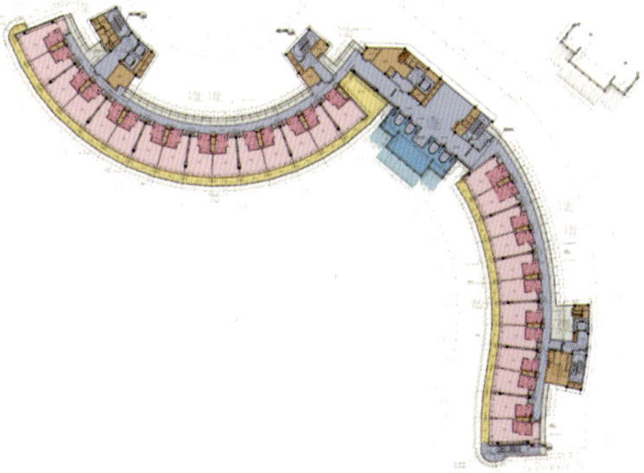

The hotel was originally conceived in 2012 by British architect Martin Jochman, who established Studio JADE & QA in Shanghai. A blueprint for the rejuvenation of abandoned quarries and industrial sites everywhere, Jochman's masterful adaptation in conforming his vision to the site's unique topography has the potential to become an international beacon for environmentally conscious travellers. It also takes the much-used term of 'adaptive re-use' – the addition of a contemporary extension to an existing and usually older structure – to an entirely new and unheard-of level: the marrying of human inventiveness and our ravaged environment.

The hotel is expecting to welcome a numbing 500,000 visitors a year, such is the audacious nature of its scale and setting. And for those who only plan a day visit there will be no shortage of activities to keep them entertained, whether it be architecture, engineering, interior design, and outdoor pursuits such as rock climbing and bungee-jumping. Jochman told the architecture magazine *Dezeen* that the building was inspired and determined by the quarry itself, and that the 'natural environment needed to be finely balanced', employing the principles of the Chinese concept of yin and yang. The quarry and the hotel would exist as distinct and inseparable opposites, with each form having at its core an element of the other.

The number of site-specific challenges the project presented are too numerous to mention. There were issues regarding fire escapes and flooding issues, as well as how to secure the hotel against rock falls. An embankment has been constructed around the quarry's edge to prevent a nearby river from flooding and filling the quarry – and the lower levels of the hotel – with water, while the water that now forms its mirror-like lake is now a permanent, regulated feature of the quarry, kept at a safe minimum level thanks to a purpose-built pump house. Thousands of engineers, architects, designers

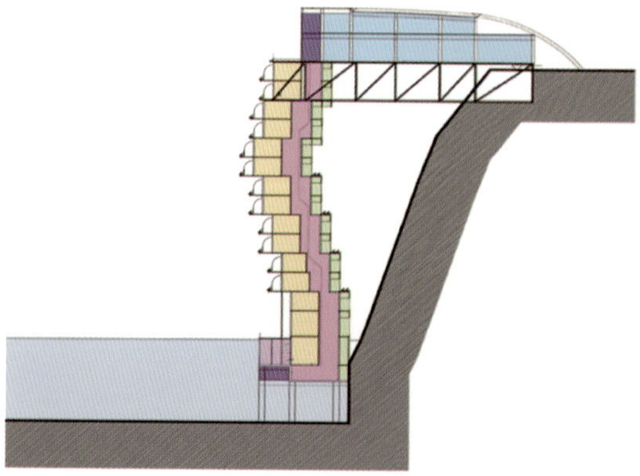

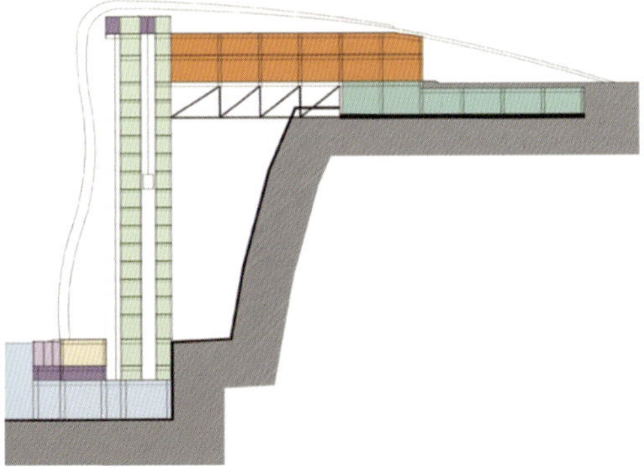

and construction workers took six years to bring it all to fruition. Concrete had to be poured downwards over 260 feet without its constituent sand and cement separating along the way. The volume of surrounding rock is used to help regulate its internal temperature, and there were seismic challenges to overcome too – the sort of challenges engineers and architects of more 'traditional' buildings rarely have to deal with. This resulted in engineering processes having to be developed which involved the filing of an astonishing 39 patents.

The hotel's adornments are breathtaking and include a glass-bottomed staircase constructed along the quarry's rockface. Even the hotel's ventilation is a product of its unique location: the cooler air at the lake surface is brought inside, and is warmed by the presence of people and the hotel's public spaces as it rises through the building, creating natural circulation. The building's anchor, the rock face of the quarry, also alternately protrudes into the building, a natural thermal mass that brings in additional natural cooling. The team has taken what had once been a blight the city could do nothing but live with, and through the magic of architecture transformed it into its brightest jewel.

D. TOUR SIGNAL

CHAPTER 6

Citadel University Campus

Amiens, France

Renzo Piano Building Workshops

There's a lot to like about the city of Amiens, 74.5 miles north of Paris. It still has its medieval belfries intact, there are the quaint cobblestoned streets of the Quartier Saint-Leu, and the 13th century Amiens Cathedral is France's largest Gothic church with the greatest internal volume of any French cathedral including Notre Dame. The Museum of Fine Arts has works by Picasso and Mirõ, and the author Jules Verne (*Journey to the Centre of the Earth*) lived here. Amiens is also a university town with one of the largest university hospitals in the country. And it was in the spirit of keeping Amiens as a centre of learning and research that the Italian architect Renzo Piano was approached and asked to redefine one of the city's most prized pieces of historic real estate – its 17th century pentagonal defensive citadel, now better known, thanks to Piano's creative genius, as the Citadel University Campus.

The citadel is a pentagonal defensive fort, commissioned by Henri IV and designed by the great mathematician and military engineer Jean Errard de Bar-le-Duc. Completed in 1622 it spreads over a prominent area of the city along the northern bank of the river Somme. Long occupied by the military who only allowed public access to the site in 1993, it became subject to an architectural competition which Piano won, and no time was lost in developing a concept for its overall redevelopment, with the goal to restore the citadel and give it back the prominence it once had at the heart of the city.

Its conversion and restoration of its three historic gates, as well as the opening of two additional access points to the east has created a vast area of interplay between the city and its northern quarters. In addition to the converted university buildings there are two restaurants, two cafes, and open spaces capable of hosting events such as concerts and an open-air cinema. Its new 500-seat auditorium can also be used for theatrical productions and concerts.

Two of the citadel's five original bastions were demolished in the 1960s to make way for the Avenue du Général de Gaulle, and Piano thought these were alterations enough, barely changing the exteriors of the main buildings and instead pouring all of his 21st

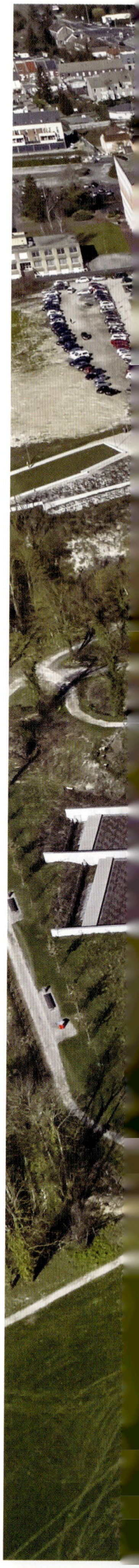

century modernist muscle into the funky futuristic red-topped tower that now rises above the Places d'Armes.

The site's complex collection of structures were added one by one over the centuries, and the project called for the demolition of some of the buildings that were deemed to be of lesser historic value. The restoration would centre on the stables and the barracks, the two major structures dating from the 19th century, and the restoration of other classified buildings including the Governor's Lodge which sits over the original Porte Montrescu, its 1390s city gate. The parade ground is the heart of this new space. Conceived as a meeting point it's bookended to the north by the barracks and to the south by the stables. The western side is bordered by the auditorium and its eastern boundary opens onto the Avenue du Général de Gaulle.

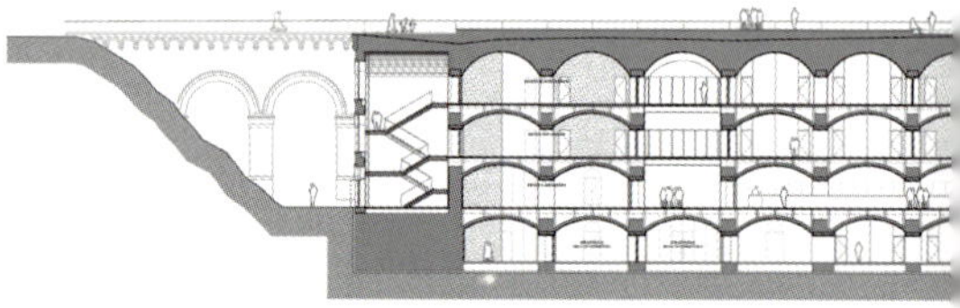

The surface of the new square includes the innovative use of extruded terracotta, its joints filled with a mixture of crushed stone and earth, each terracotta strip separated by thin inch-wide strips of grass to create a self-draining palette. On this foundation rests Piano's flight of fancy, the 'signal' building, its three superimposed boxes stacked one atop the other with a restaurant on its ground floor and containing five lecture halls. The smallest of the boxes is the striking red cube, a periscope-like metal box which looks out over the city's grand cathedral and the Tour Perret, the 360 foot-high, 27 story commercial building made from reinforced concrete and one of Europe's very first 'skyscrapers', completed in 1954 and designed by Belgian architect Auguste Perret.

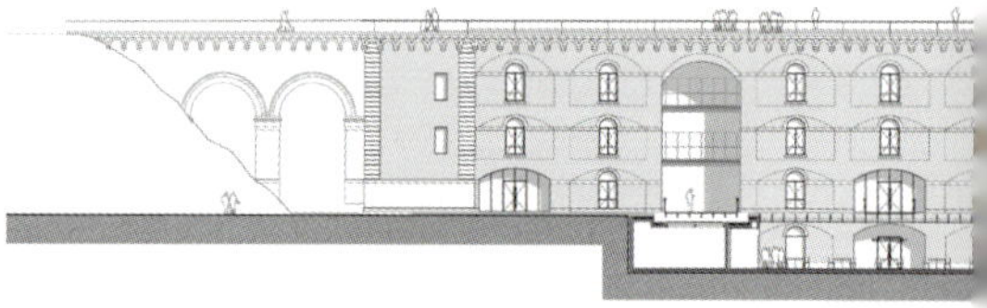

The material used on the square is also present to the north on the roof of the former barracks, thus converting it into a vast viewing platform 377 feet long, open to everyone and providing panoramic views across the city. On the ground floor of the old barracks is the library, its interior illuminated from above via a large glazed roof along

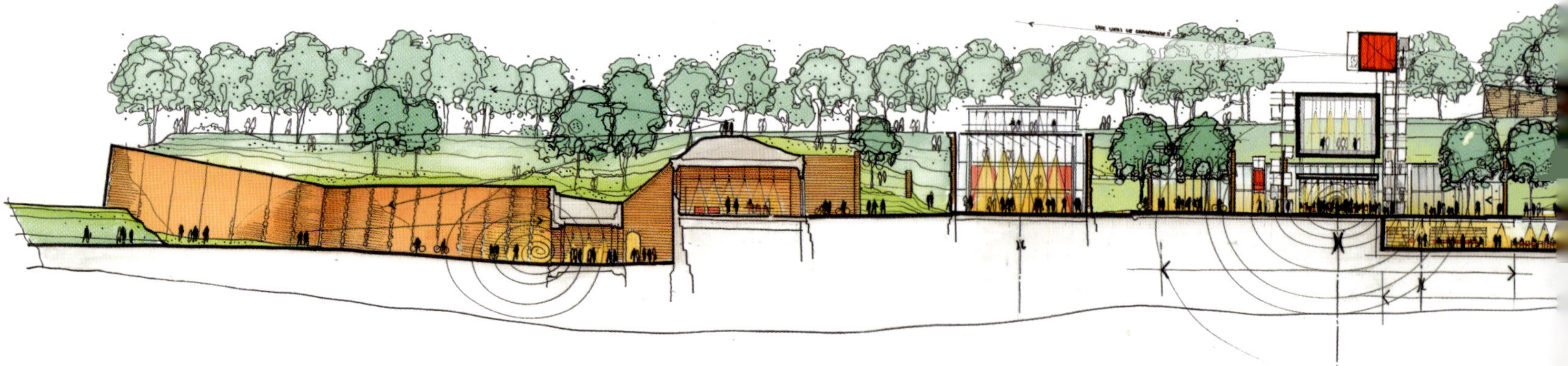

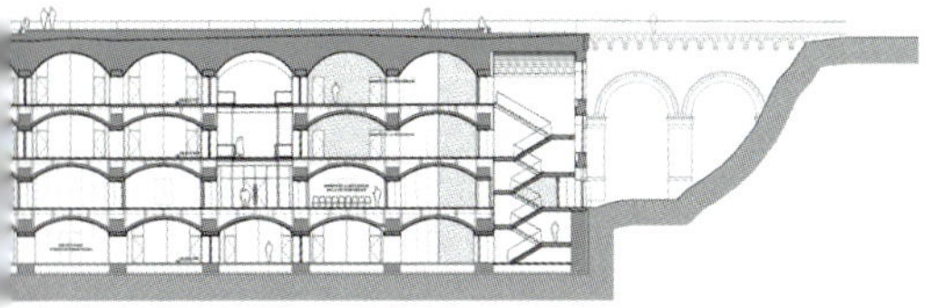

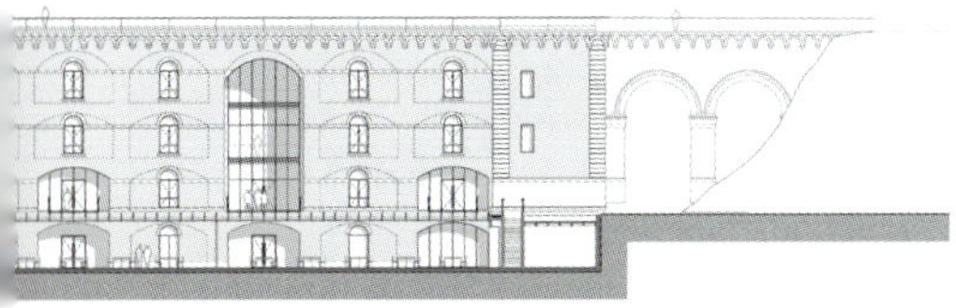

its southern façade. A student restaurant is on the ground floor and opens to the square.

The barracks' façades have been cleaned, and this impressive building is now traversed by two passageways. The east-facing passageway provides access to the mostly glassed-in street that joins it on three levels to the three northern pavilions, which are equipped with a series of automated openings to provide ventilation, the structure with its terracotta and concrete composite floor supported by a steel post and beam frame. The pre-fabricated floor uses 26 foot-long sections of half-barrel, vault-shaped terracotta extrusions held together by a cast-concrete beam through their centre. The west-facing passage provides access to a landscaped walkway and on to a footbridge that takes you over the moat and on to the sports centre on the site's northern plateau beyond the fortified perimeter.

The stables' already generous volumes have been converted into classrooms, while a set-back attic floor replaces the original pitched roof. The building has been extended beyond a covered courtyard and is now used as space for administrative offices. The buildings wonderful timber joists that had been hidden in its floor were again revealed and brought back to life, and its interior lit courtesy of large glazed façades akin to those of the northern pavilions.

A large public park now lies within the citadel's bastions and curtain walls, occupying the highest part of the ramparts, and a promenade is now accessed via ramps and elevators. The base of the ramparts, alongside the citadel's defensive moats are also now park-like thanks to an extensive program of replanting to encourage biodiversity.

The converted citadel opened its doors to students in September 2018. What Jean Errard de Bar-le-Duc tried to make impregnable, Renzo Piano has enshrined as a new and dynamic addition to one of France's must-see cities.

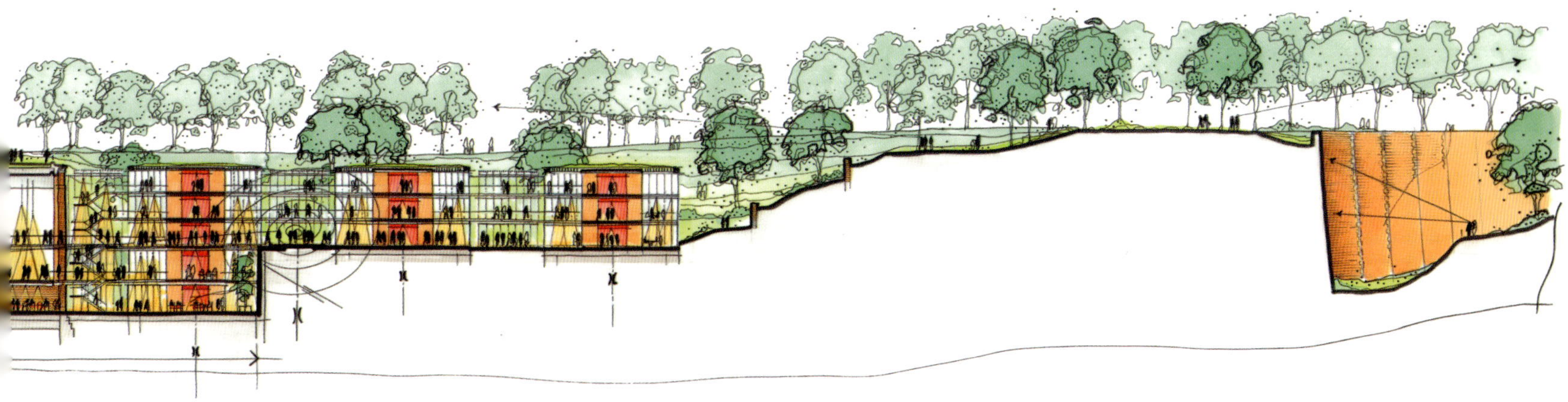

UNIVERSITÉ
DE PICARDIE

CHAPTER 7

La Valletta City Gate

Valletta, Malta

Renzo Piano Building Workshops

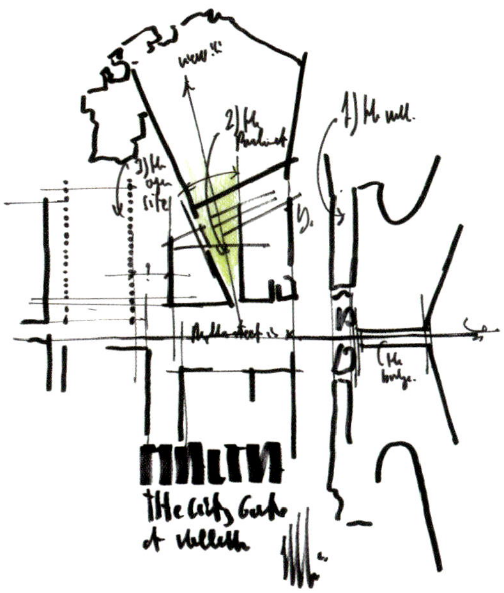

During World War II the Mediterranean island of Malta became one of Europe's most-bombed places. Strategically located between Europe and North Africa it was a staging post for Allied supply convoys with more than 3000 bombing raids over two years by the German and Italian air forces reducing large portions of the capital, Valletta, to rubble. This included the Royal Opera House, built between 1862 and 1866 by the English architect Edward Barry, destroyed in a bombardment on 7 April 1942.

Since then its ruins have been treasured by local Maltese as though they were some long lost archaeological remains; battered fragments of Malta's collective memory. Then came the 'City Gate' project, a bold vision of the Maltese government to transform the entrance to the World Heritage-listed Old Town. The Royal Opera House site would become an open-air theatre, a brand new parliament building would be constructed, and the city's famous City Gate would be given new life. It was a grand vision that would transform the Old Town's main point of entry for generations to come.

Thousands of patriotic Maltese citizens were furious at the thought of it – hardly a surprise when you consider Malta is the European Union's most densely populated country where town planning is scrutinized like nowhere else. The proposed changes to the gate – which is not the original gate built in 1569 but a brutal 1960s reconfiguration, the fifth gate to be built on the site – would bring intolerable volumes of traffic into the city's medieval streets, opponents said. Many also thought that the city already had open-air theaters aplenty, and that an actual opera house, along the lines of what had stood before, was needed. The new parliament was thought an example of architectural vanity. Opposition to the proposed changes united people across the island's social and political spectrum.

Delivering a design that would minimize the outrage would be no mean feat.

The project involved four distinct stages: the Valletta City Gate and its site immediately outside the defensive walls, the open-air theatre on the site of the former opera house, the new Parliament, and the landscaping of the defensive ditch. The bridge, leading across the ditch to the City Gate, was the project's 'funnel'. Repeatedly

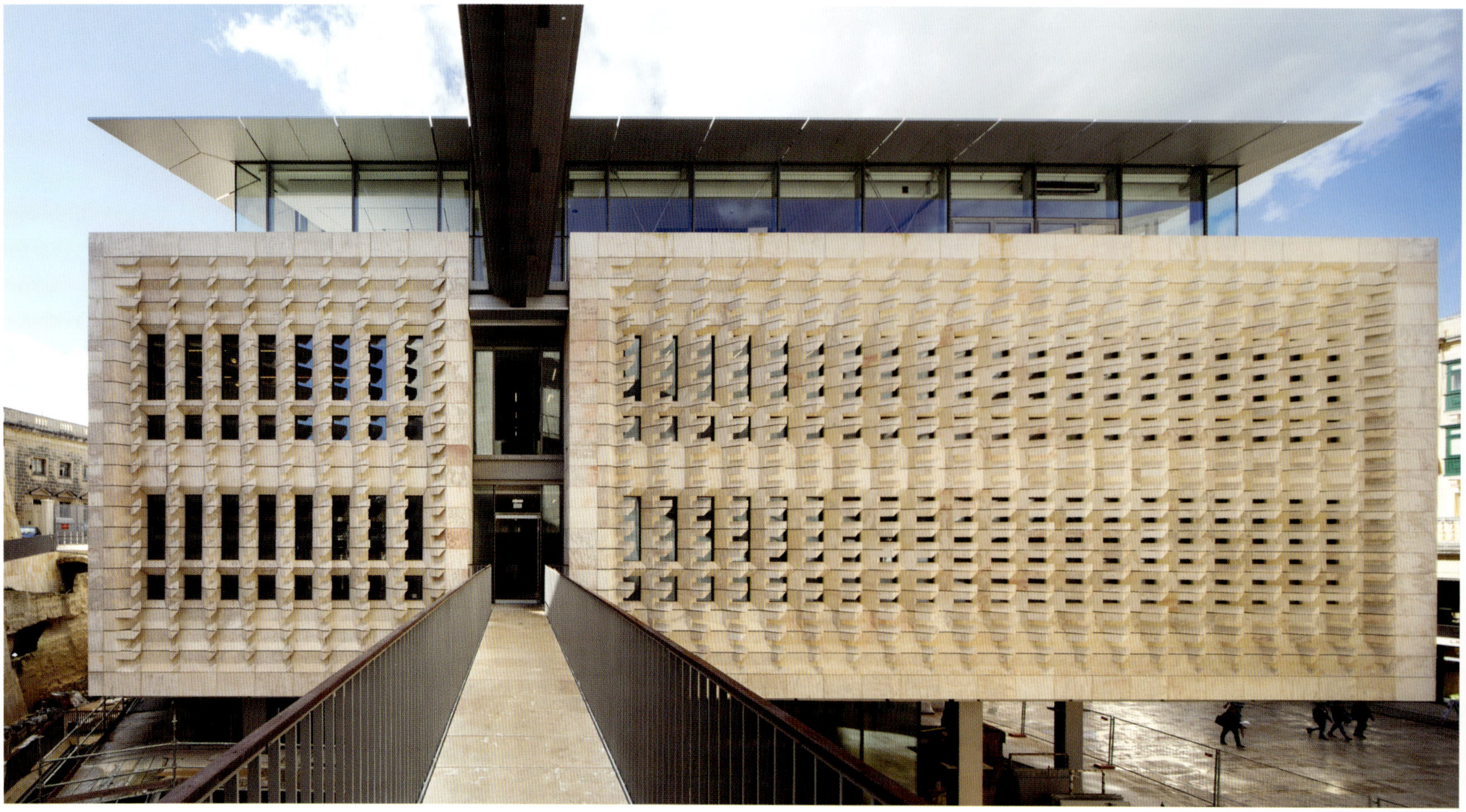

enlarged over the centuries it had long since lost all semblance to its initial shape and function, becoming more gathering place than bridge. To resolve this the 60 foot wide bridge would be radically overhauled, reducing its width back to the 1633 dimensions given it by its Maltese-born architect and sculptor Tomasso Dingli, to give pedestrians the feel that they were, in fact, on a bridge, while at the same time expanding views over the defensive ditch below and the city's fortifications above.

One of the project's primary goals was to restore the fortifications' overwhelming sense of depth and volume by reconfiguring the entrance to the city, reducing it in scale to an 26 foot 'breach'. The opening up of the new gate to the sky was achieved with the demolition of a raised section of Pope Pius V Street which had ran inside the gate, replacing it with two wide, sloping stairways which would link the bastions of St James's Cavalier and St John's Cavalier to Republic Street. Now the fortifications could again be seen in their full glory. The gate and ditch would be linked via a stairway and a lift that would take visitors from the ramparts down into the bowels of the defensive ditch, formerly used as a car park but now planted out with the final piece in the 'jigsaw' of the City Gate Project: the gardens.

The architecture is thin on ornamentation, which Piano eschewed in his quest for strength and austerity; the entry to be stripped of any extraneous decoration that would undermine its timeless appearance. Its tapered shape, its masonry, and two monumental 82 ft steel poles that symbolize the coming together of the old and the new provide the gateway with all of the status it requires. A brand new 'hardstone' quarry on the nearby island of Gozo was opened specifically to provide the stone for the City Gate Project.

The new parliament building consists of two massive stone blocks balanced on slender columns that makes the building seem lighter than it is. The northernmost block contains the parliamentary chamber, while the south block provides accommodation

for the members of parliament and the offices of the Prime Minister and Opposition Leader. Both blocks are separated by a central courtyard, which is also the building's main entrance to the building, designed so to provide views through to St James's Cavalier. The building also stands separate from St James' Cavalier bastion, highlighting the latter's importance as a vital part of the city's medieval fortifications.

The pierced, fretted appearance seen on the new parliament's stone façades were inspired by the weathered stones of Malta's old Baroque and Renaissance monuments. Combined with laser-cut edging they sit out at an angle rather than being flush, hinting at the Moorish tradition that allows for glimpses into internal spaces.

The ground floor was also designed to be a flexible, multi-use cultural space, a venue for temporary or permanent art exhibits fully visible from outside. The building's basement opens onto a shaded garden courtyard which itself is connected to the old Malta railway tunnel that had been used for many years as a car park, giving it new life and once again making it accessible to the public. The extensive use of stone, combined with 40 geothermal boreholes drilled 460 ft into the bedrock (and 328 ft below sea-level) provides an effective, natural solution to the building's energy needs. When combined with the 6460 square feet of solar panels on the new parliament's roof the building generates almost 80 percent of the energy needed to warm it in winter, and more than half of the energy it requires to cool it in summer.

And what of the ruins of the Royal Opera? They have now been restored as the open-air theatre so many were wary of, faithfully integrated into the new project … and it is winning over the capital's citizens. When events are not scheduled, it functions as a piazza, a welcome open space. The mechanics of it provide it great flexibility. Around 1000 seats can be installed and the stage adapted for opera, concerts and dance: a varied program that calls for a variety of configurations that are easy to achieve thanks to the theatre's mechanical accoutrements and stage wings. An electronic Reflected Energy System (RES) acoustic enhancement system, the product of ongoing advancements in

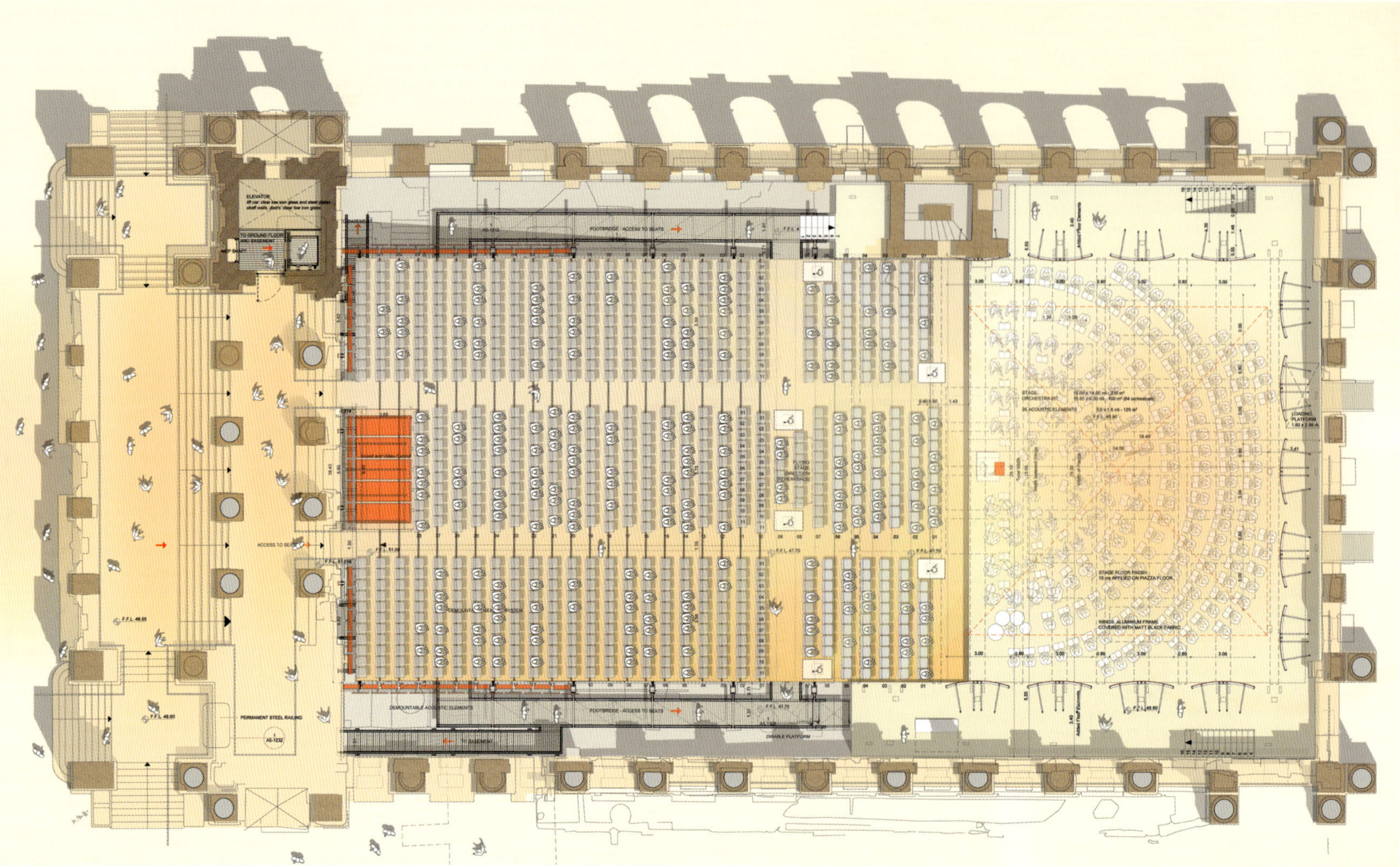
FOOTBRIDGE - ACCESS TO SEATS
DEMOUNTABLE ACOUSTIC ELEMENTS
PERMANENT STEEL RAILING

MARKEN KIOSK

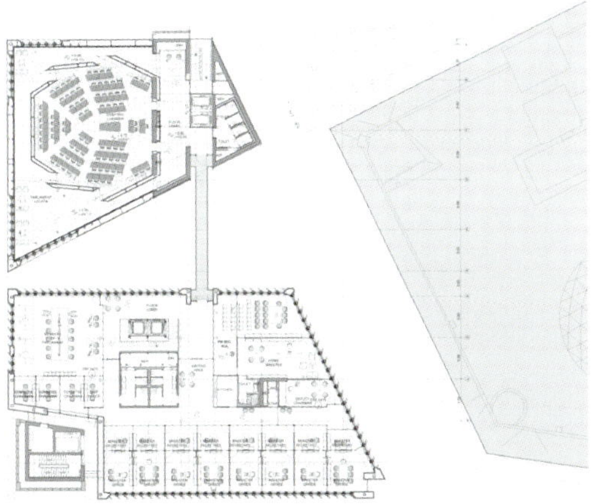

digital signal processing, has also been installed to simulate the acoustics of a large concert hall.

In the end, the ruins of the opera house were not bulldozed. Propped up with steelwork they now act as a framework for a series of translucent screens, which close vertically during performances to isolate the theatre from nearby crowded streets. 'The real sacrilege', Piano said, 'would have been to destroy those ruins. But keep them, give them dignity, give them functions, and add machines to make art – I think that's great. That's magic'.

CHAPTER 8

Centro Botín

Santander, Spain

Renzo Piano Building Workshop

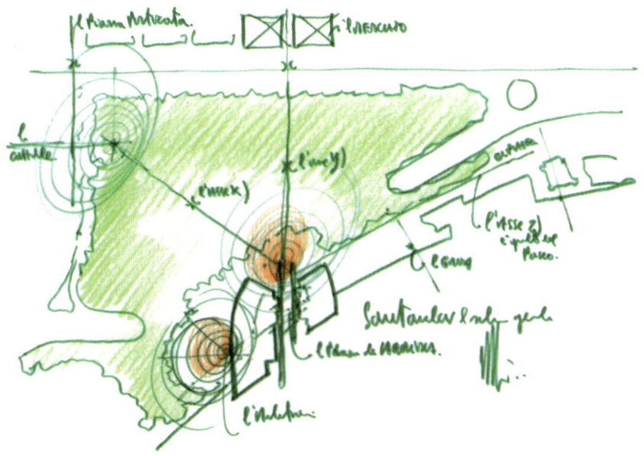

'I wanted the building to fly', Renzo Piano once said of Centro Botín. And so it seems that it might, poised on the seafront in Santander in northern Spain looking like the swept-back wings of some ungainly, mechanical seabird. But when the great Italian architect was approached to build it, locals were worried that its bulk would obliterate their views of the Cantabrian Sea. They needn't have worried. The museum would be raised up, levitating atop a network of 20 foot-high white pillars. Not only could you still see the water, you now had a choice of how much you could see. You could stand behind Centro Botín and look out from under it or, if you want to see more – much more – why not go inside and step out onto one of its external terraces? The city had been given a new vantage point.

It was Emilio Botín himself who suggested to the great Italian architect they eliminate the old coastal road – too long a blight; too long a barrier cutting off the city from its beloved bay – by placing it underground.

And why stop there? With the road gone, a commission could then be given to the renowned landscape designer Fernando Caruncho with a brief to double the size of the historic Pereda Gardens. This was, of course, sauce for the goose to Piano who loved nothing more than to facilitate the coming together of public spaces, to bring two or three or more ideas together to create something of greater consequence than the sum of its parts. What happened here on the waterfront in Santander was a cosmic 'Big Bang' of common sense town planning. And Centro Botín lit the fuse to it all.

A wholly private initiative of the Botín Foundation (Spain's most high-profile private cultural foundation) Centro Botín, on the site of what used to be the old ferry port car park, is now home to the foundation's growing collection of contemporary art, an ongoing program of temporary exhibits, and various robust cultural education programs. In addition to its extensive exhibition spaces there are conference rooms, workspaces, a shop, a rooftop terrace, 300-seat auditorium, and even a restaurant founded by the doyen of local Cantabrian cuisine and Michelin-starred chef, Jésus Sánchez.

Its two D-shaped blocks, curving volumes of structural glazing and stainless steel,

are joined by a network of interconnected stairways and gantries that zigzag their way up to the building's rooftop terrace. Everything is oriented to, and given meaning by, the bay over which it sits – a fact that Piano delighted in exploiting. 'Salty water is my natural habitat' he said while present at its opening in 2017. He was determined that his building, when completed, would 'flirt' with the water.

The 270,000 exuberant pearl-colored, ceramic discs that clad its exterior surfaces, which look a little like a vast expanse of glittering barnacles, were chosen for two reasons. Firstly because ceramics are such a part of the history of Spain; secondly because their curved form enhances the reflecting of light, so much so that even on a grey Santander day they impart a rare elegance. But more than anything else, Piano wanted the building to be a place for people to meet, to be together – and to be a place of change. Beauty, art, understanding and knowledge – Piano believes exposure to these things change people, they make us better. The building is as much an expression of his belief in what it means to be human as it is a place to display and encourage the pursuit of art.

Not far from Santander in the old port city of Bilbao, Frank Gehry's Guggenheim has put the old port city on the map; its presence so pervasive, so transforming that it's even led to the birth of a new architectural phrase: the Bilbao Effect. Will Piano's entrancing combination of subtlety and grandeur do the same here? Time will tell. It may be less of an imposition on the city's landscape, it might make less of a 'fuss', but its creators were never interested in showing off. Santander is a small place with a population of just 170,000, and more conservative than busy, bustling Bilbao.

But make no mistake. All the architectural and cultural ingredients reside here in one glorious package. Central Botín is already writing its own story.

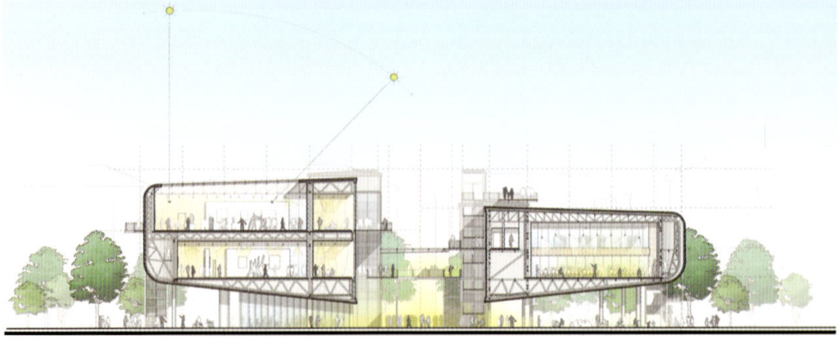

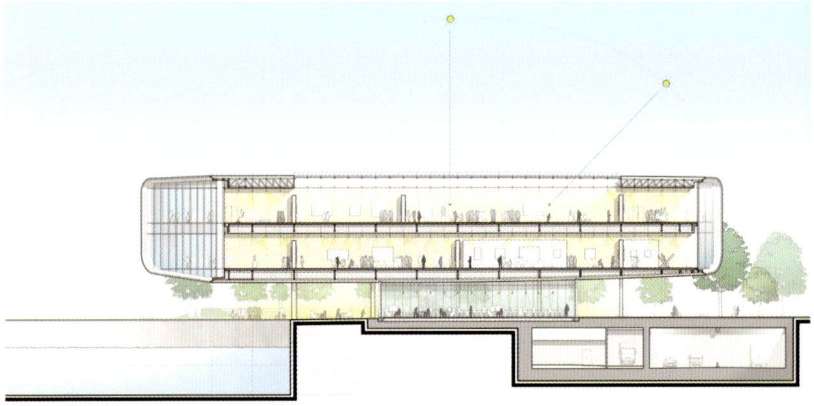

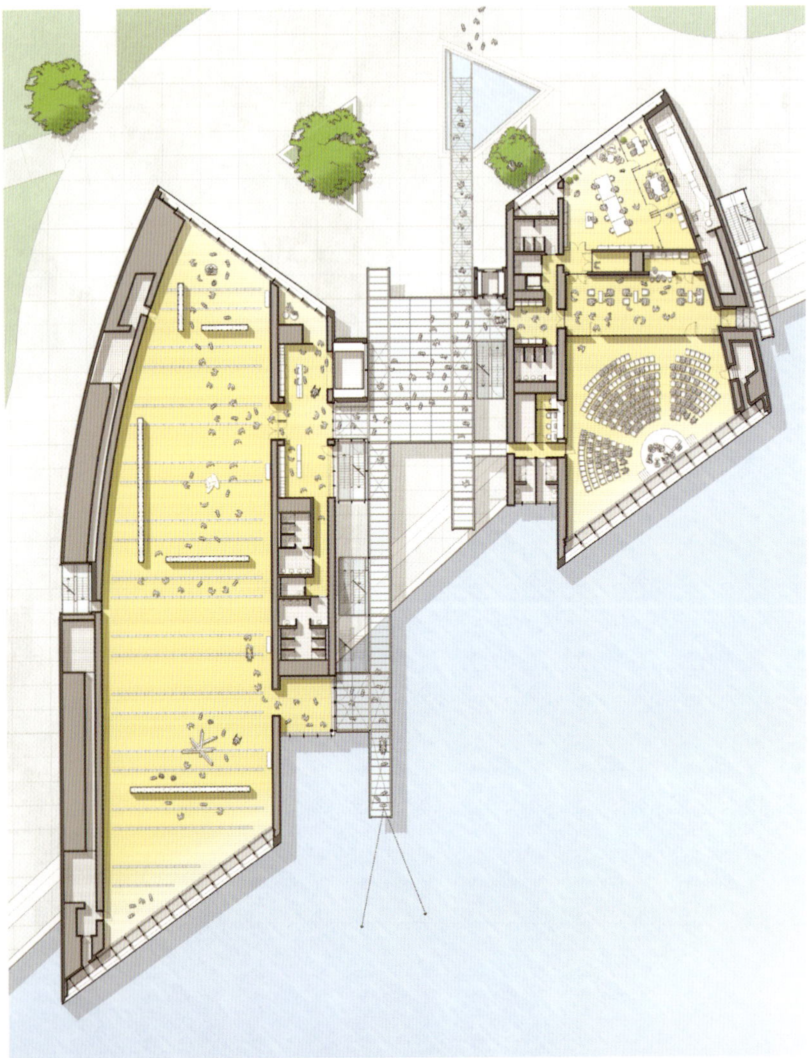

CHAPTER 9

Harbin Opera House

Harbin, China

MAD Architects

Few building types symbolise a nation's economic coming of age quite like a skyscraper. They heralded a new can-do era in American industry when they began to alter the skylines of Chicago and New York in the 1930s, and such a transformation is happening again today in China, which will be home to more than 20 of the world's 50 tallest buildings by the end of 2020. China's love affair with tall buildings is a testament to its burgeoning economy, its growing international relevance, and are a reflection of the heightened aspirations of an increasingly wealthy populace. But height isn't everything. In fact it's ironic, perhaps, that the building which, many argue, has done more to highlight China's new era of prosperity and sophistication isn't tall at all. It doesn't have to be. And you only have to look at it to know why.

MAD Architect's Harbin Opera House is one of the most inspiring new buildings on the planet. Sculpturally sublime, breathtaking, a force of nature – critics have run out of superlatives in their attempts to convey its majesty. Rising out of the surrounding wetlands is 850,350 square feet of pure zen and the centrepiece of the city's new Art Hub, an attempt by MAD's founding principal Ma Yansong to blend the building into the very horizon itself, gaining inspiration from the water that flows along the area's riverbanks to create a grand architectural statement. From the air it resembles a white dragon sitting in – but not born of – the landscape, a building whose crescent, looping form owes its very existence to the natural features that embrace it.

Rather than imposing itself upon the landscape, rather than soaring above it, MAD's opera house radiates a soothing aesthetic. It's a building that is always open, regardless of whether there's a performance or not . . . and it can even be walked on, with a stairway of granite steps that takes you onto the roof to a platform that provides views over the city and the nearby Songhua River. 'I wanted people to be able to climb the building, like a mountain', Ma likes to say. More than anything else the goal was to create *atmosphere* in a building that champions light, space and form. It's all such a triumph, in fact, that you'd be forgiven for worrying the music might play second fiddle to the building that was designed to show it off. But MAD never lost sight of the building's function.

Inside, the 1600-seat Grand Theatre resembles a gargantuan snow cave. Its walls are awash in Manchurian ash, parts of which are solid wood cladding, other parts thin quarter-inch veneers attached to fibreglass and concrete. Its transparent glass roof is held aloft by a honeycomb-like façade of striking white aluminium panels that sheath its curvilinear exterior In addition to the Grand Theatre, with its deep orchestra pit and expansive backstage spaces that provide for the largest of large-scale theatrical and musical productions, there's also a smaller 400-seat theatre as well as the all the necessary rehearsal rooms, dressing rooms, and other multifunctional spaces.

For a building with such gigantic proportions there's a lot to be admired in its details. Its glass walls and skylights are engineered to melt snow and direct the run-off into purpose-built drains. The undulating Manchurian Ash that embraces the stage of the Grand Theatre has been curved to resemble the interior of a musical instrument, wood that flows like water which took a team of 50 artisans four months to complete. All around you a serpentine labyrinth of staircases packs a not-to-be-forgotten visual punch. The gloriously curved precast concrete walls in the foyer and public areas funnel internal circulation, and the marble in its floors is integrated with an underfloor heating system to combat winter temperatures that can plummet to as low as minus 38 degrees Celcius.

Home to China's famous annual Harbin Snow Festival, this northern Chinese city on the borderlands close to Russia has long given it the feel of a frontier town with all of the uncertainty that being at the crossroads of east and west entails. Now the city, albeit with its ageing European core, has been put firmly on the world's architectural map. Through it, Harbin can reinvent itself, use it as a beacon through which to showcase its heritage and identity. That might seem an improbable goal in such a faraway place. But surely no more improbable than building an opera house in the middle of a wetland on the low-lying side of a flood prone river?

'When humans go into an environment', says Ma Yansong, 'whether artificial or natural, they feel something. That's the reason we talk about context . . . I'd say this place has a very strong character. On the edge of a river that is very special. It's very wide, and if you look from the air, it's shape is very organic. When I saw this, I thought this would be a strong pathway towards understanding this place'.

And finally, in a world where architecture can often come across as over-engineered and impersonal, here is a building which, despite being a product of CAD, feels far removed from mathematical algorithms. Its wood gives it a hand-crafted quality while at the same time preserving the 'new', a sense of the abstract that has made for a perfect fusion of imagination, ingenuity and hope.

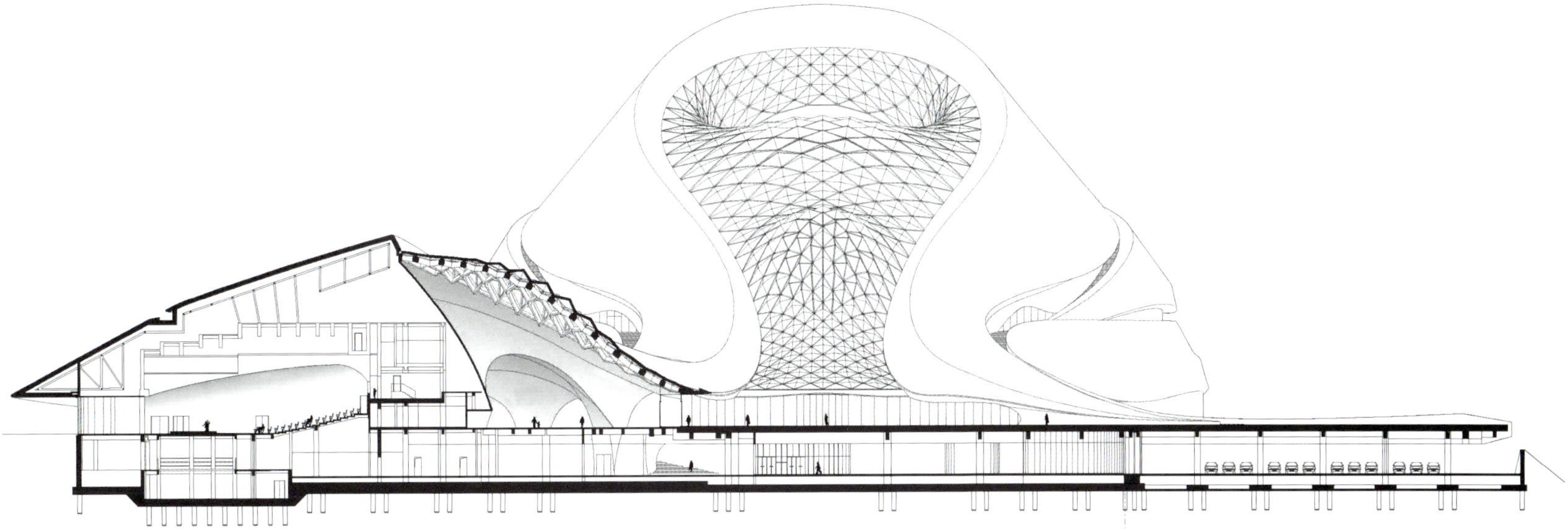

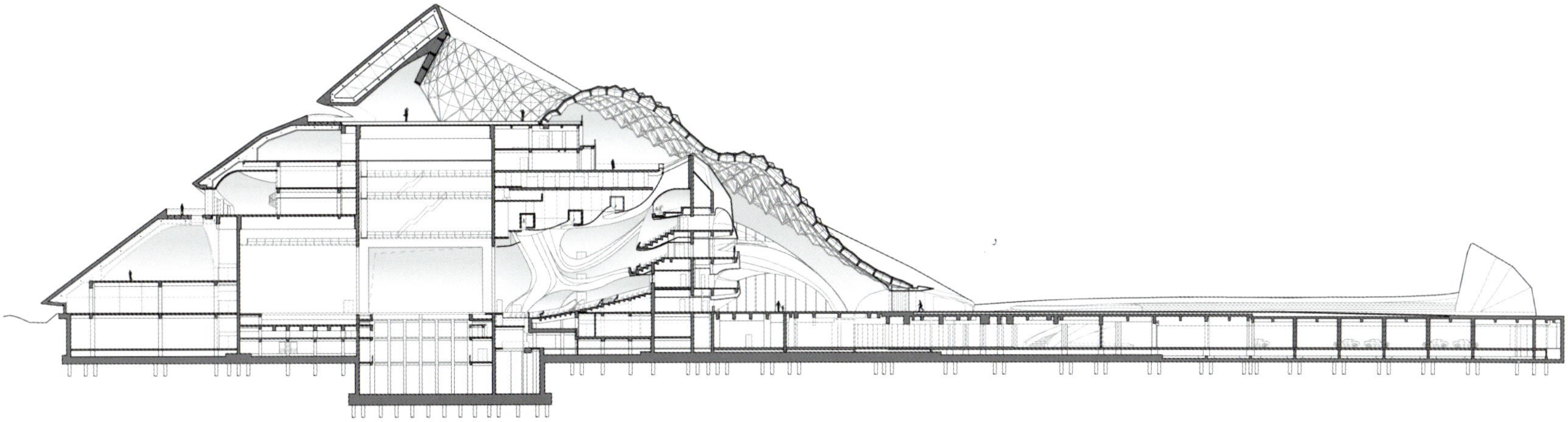

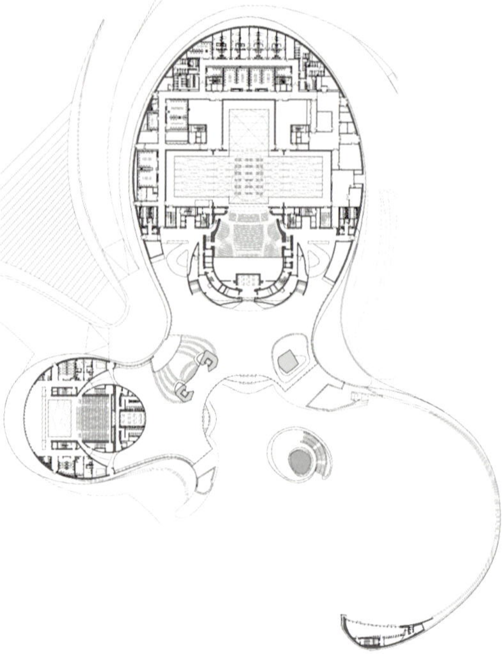
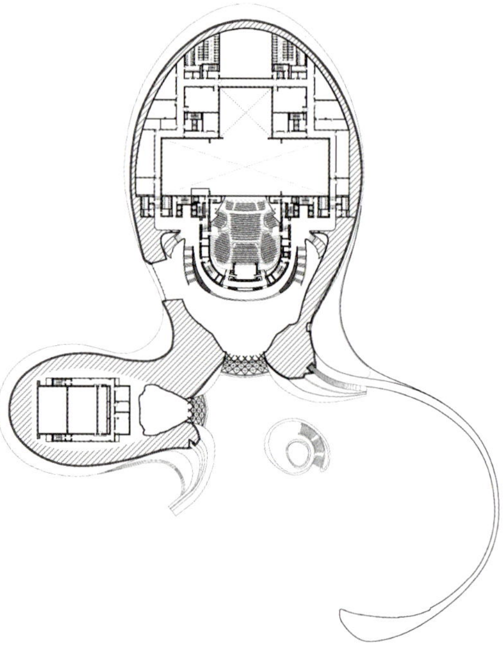
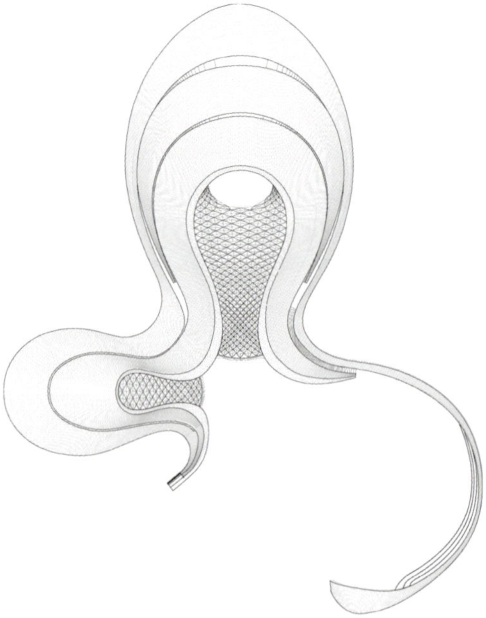

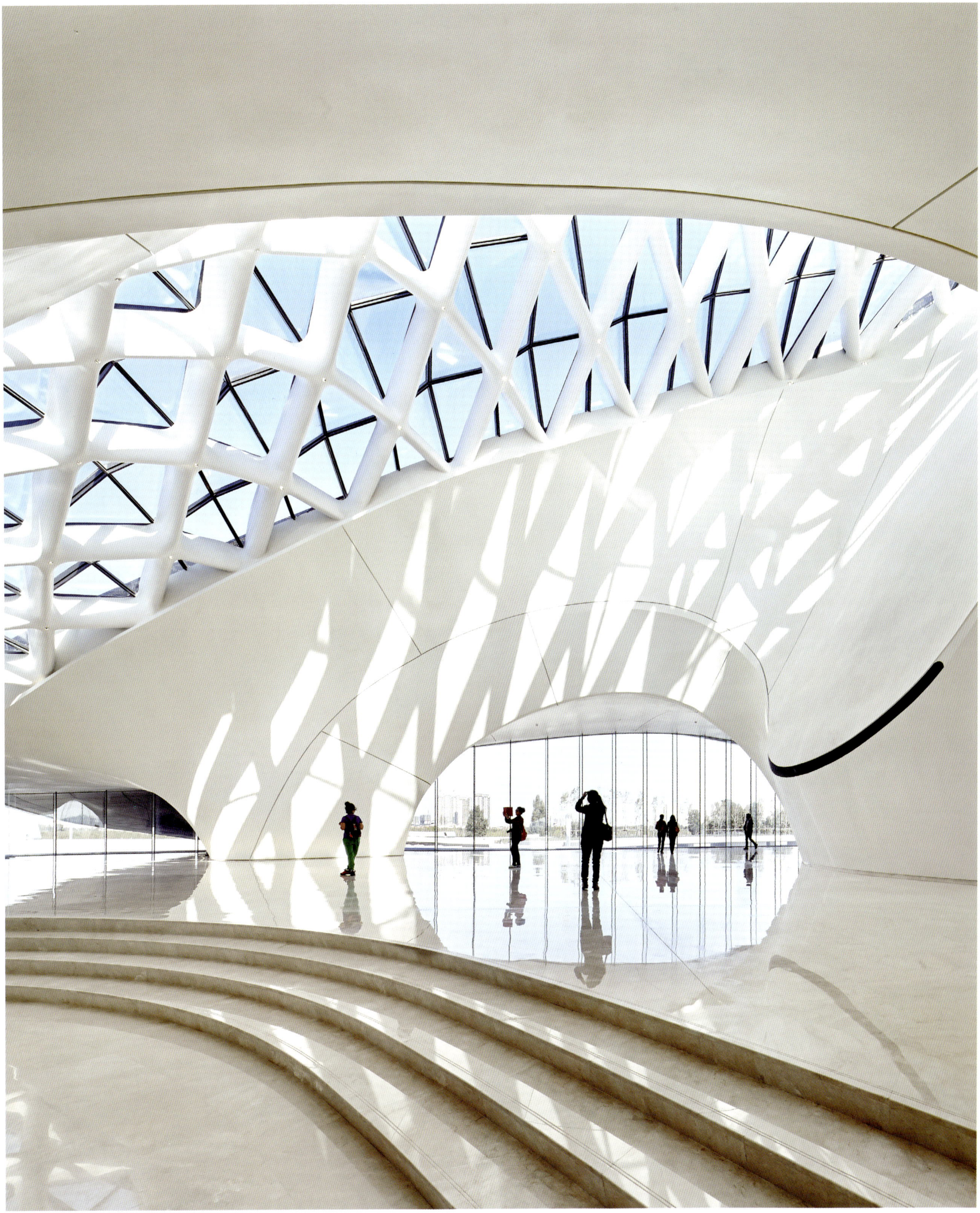

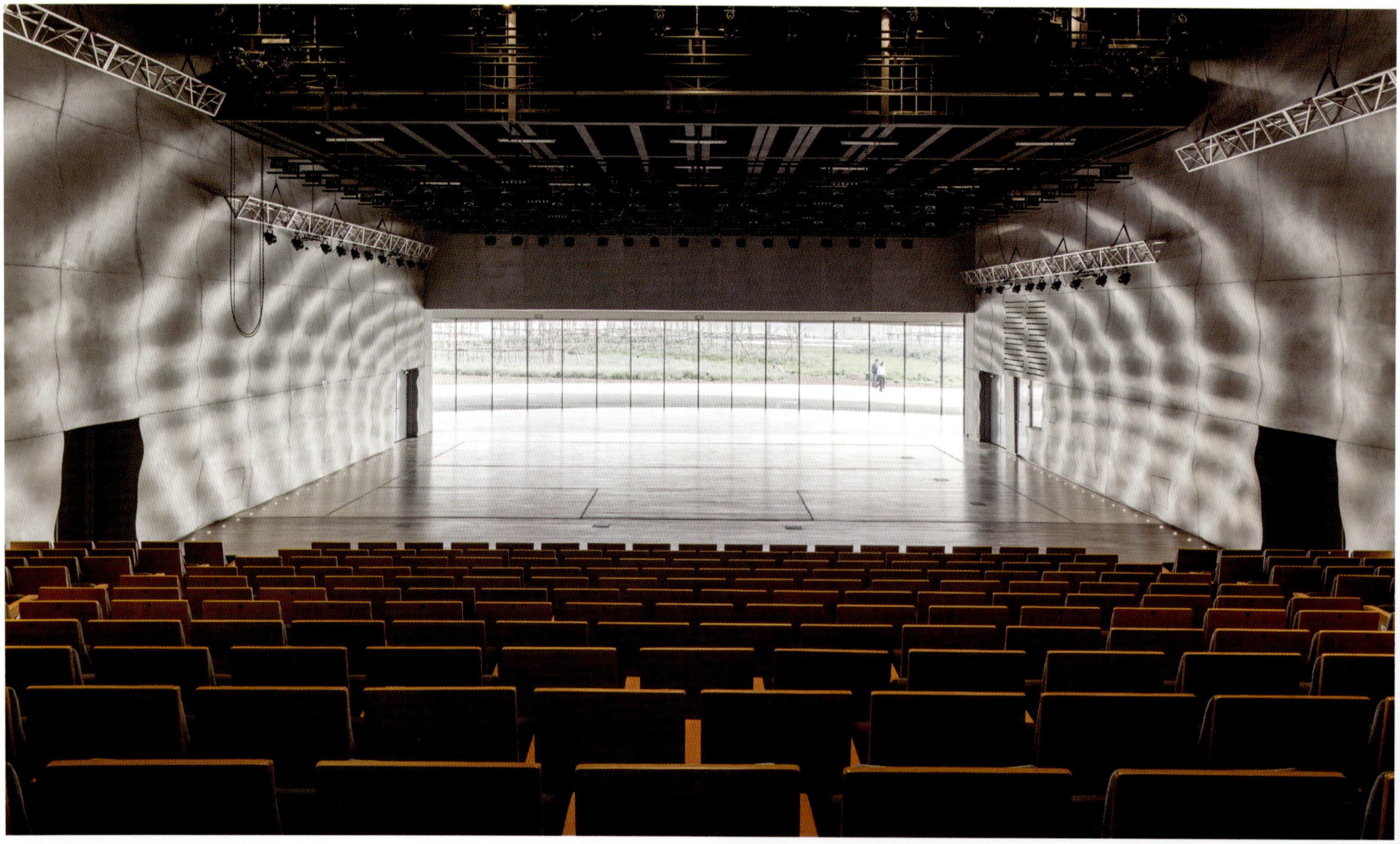

Burlington St

CHAPTER 10

Voxman Music Building

Iowa City, USA

LMN Architects

At every turn a celebration of the gift of music, the Voxman Music Building, part of the University of Iowa in Iowa City in the United States, replaced an earlier building of the same name which was destroyed by flood waters in 2008. With a sumptuously composed and subtly-layered mix of low-iron glass and reflective terracotta panels, the exterior shimmers with confidence, its interior a sensitive, considered mix of impeccably planned and acoustically independent spaces. It provides teachers, students and visitors with a venue that borders on the flawless in its pursuit of the perfect musical realm.

The site (which in its first incarnation was an old drive-through bank prior to the first Voxman building being raised in the early 1960s) is at the intersection of Clinton and Burlington at the edge of this vibrant campus and straddles the boundary of Iowa City's bustling downtown – an ideal meeting point of learning and commerce. The idea was to build a transparent corner at that intersection, a building with carefully positioned glass façades that would invite the city in and allow passers by to glimpse its interior, to pique their interest … in other words, to entice the public to come to its concerts.

The building's compact footprint, just 30,000 square feet, meant it was always going to be tall – 6½ storys tall – a challenge in aitself because acoustic spaces don't generally like being 'stacked' upon each other. But LMN Architects did their reputation for creating community-focused civic projects no harm at all in designing a technological tour-de-force here. The building is filled with embedded technologies and acoustic innovations that made the difficult possible. So determined were LMN to create something new here that a ⅓ scale mock-up was built to test the methods and materials the architects were interested in deploying, and to assist them in all of the processes of acoustic analysis in the refining of its spaces. Built with a parametric model and a CNC machine with a 4 x 8 CNC router, cutouts were made in the model's aluminium composite parts that were also scored along their reverse sides to create tabs that could be folded back by hand so the model could be easily assembled.

The Voxman Music Building's 700-seat concert hall is a traditional 'shoebox' design that incorporates a revolutionary, suspended 'theatroacoustic' system, a gorgeous undulating surface that is certainly the building's crown jewel, bringing together in one unified expression of architecture all of the room's lighting, acoustics, and line-safety elements as well as sprinklers, speakers and catwalks. Composed of 946 folded, individually crafted aluminium acoustic panels they were created by the innovative LMN Tech Studio, all digitally fabricated thanks to the mock-up model. The building's three ensemble rooms are all covered in variants of these cloud-like assemblages – normally used on external façades but installed here in an origami-like approach to the pursuit of acoustic perfection.

The centrepiece of the concert hall is its magnificent Klais Organ, with its almost 4000 pipes and guaranteed by the Klais Organ Company in Germany for the next 200 years. Unlike the building's 140 or so pianos, an instrument that has remained more or less static for generations, the organ has been continuously evolving over the centuries. And once they get this big there are no two alike. There's nothing quite like it anywhere in America – an instrument so large it even has its own internal spiral staircase so students can gain an appreciation of its complex mechanics.

The 200-seat Recital Hall, with its jewel-like scarlet wall of customized acoustic panels which surely makes it one of the most beautiful internal walls in America has a 29.5 foot-high wall of glass which opens the stage to the public. A rarity for any performance space to abut so much glass, the wall brought its own set of acoustic challenges: namely the infiltration of noise. To reduce external noise, two layers of inch thick laminated glass, separated by a three inch air cavity, were used. The glass was laid horizontally, an architectural 'trick' that reduces sound distortion by lessening its tendency to vibrate. The scarlet panels are exquisite; composed of glass fibre reinforced gypsum (GFRG), their mix of surfaces diffusing sound for a fuller acoustic experience.

The building is a triumph of functionality, with acoustic flourishes everywhere. Felt panels were installed into the extra-thick cast in place concrete of the student rooms, reducing the concrete's natural tendency to echo. And the student rooms are just a few

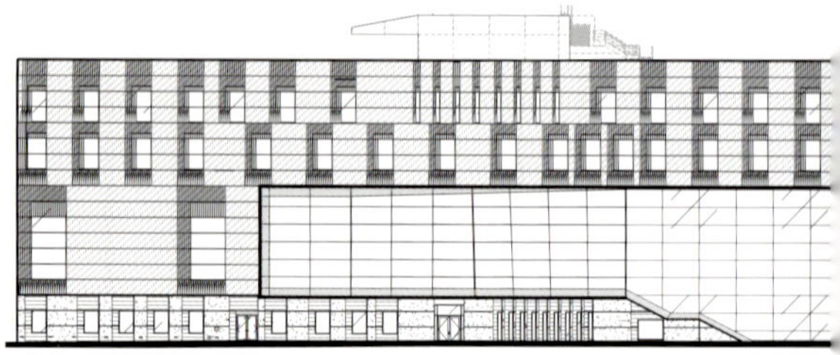

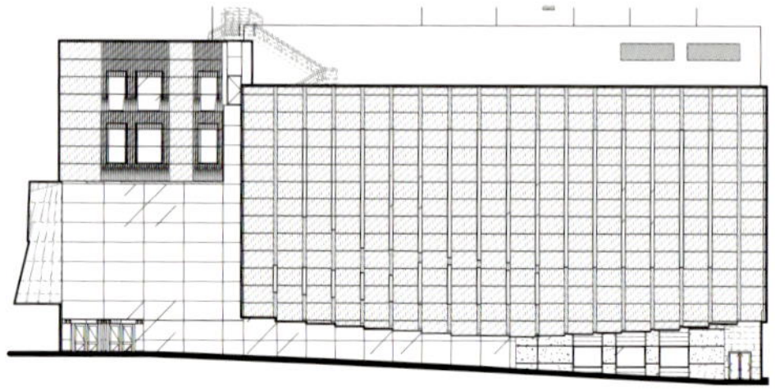

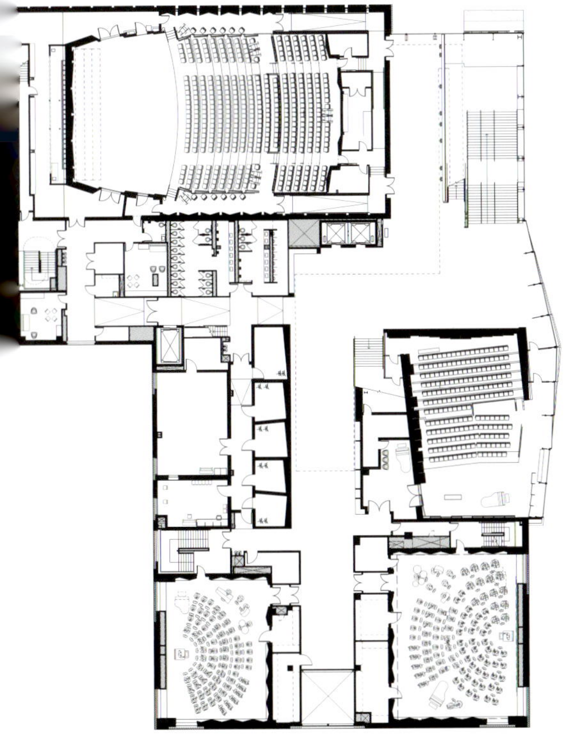

of the array of rooms here – there's a total of 65 practise rooms alone. It also includes an organ recital hall, opera studio, various orchestral rooms, teaching rooms, a library, a rare book room and electronic music suites. These help deliver on every aspect, every nuance in the learning, playing and appreciation of music, from the study of its theory to concert hall formality and public space improvisation.

It's hard to know what to be more excited about, its meticulously crafted interior or stunning exterior. Part of its second floor exterior bulges outward to add volume to the recital hall, its surface set at varying angles which both improves the internal acoustics and provides a lovely shingled look from the street. The horizontal bands of its external terracotta 'rainscreen' are a combination of glazed, unglazed, scored and smooth finishes. The 90-degree tiles were the first to ever be used on a façade in the United States, the product of 12 months of research and development. What's more their creation was refreshingly old-fashioned: the result of hand-pressing clay into moulds prior to being air dried and then kiln fired.

Throughout the Voxman Music Building there is an abundance of light, natural light that enters through its apertures and extensive glazed surfaces regardless of the time of day, light in all its various guises and perspectives. All the better to illuminate all of the obvious – and the not so obvious – details of this wonderful testament to humankind's musical mind.

CONCERT HALL

CONCERT HALL

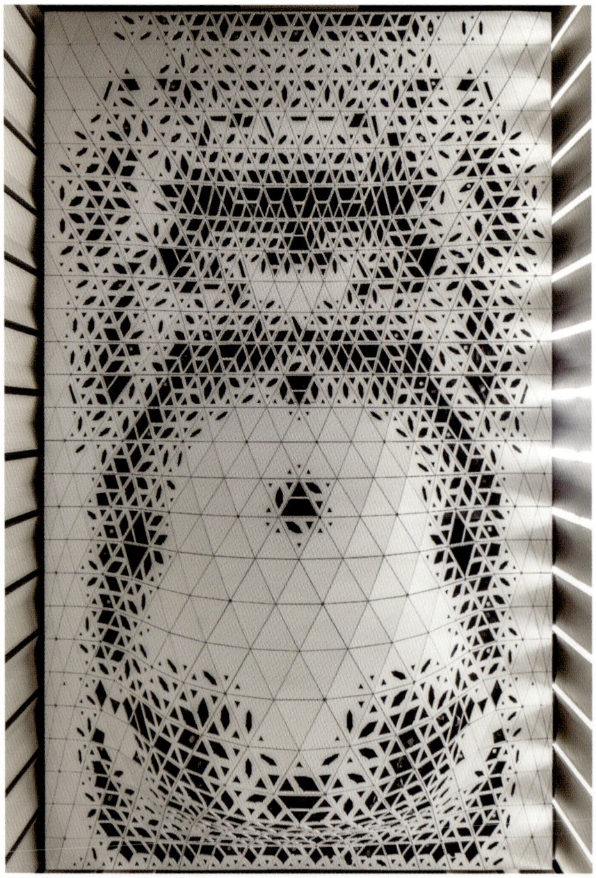

CHAPTER 11

Nanjing Zendai Himalayas Centre

Nanjing, China

MAD Architects

Take a look at MAD Architect's new Nanjing Zendai Himalayas Centre in the city of Nanjing in eastern China, and all sorts of things come to mind, most of them in the realm of pop culture. One thinks of movies like The Fifth Element and Bladerunner, of futuristic neon-lit cities with dense urban cores surrounded by towering skyscrapers. Nanjing Zendai certainly looks to be a world within itself, a self-contained metropolis that must have been seen almost as a folly to some when a large scale installation of it all was first unveiled at the Venice Architecture Biennale in 2014.

Now here it is at last, fully realized in all its futuristic glory, a multi-use development of apartments, offices, hotels and shops that tower around the perimeter of this ambitious precinct. And at its heart, not so much as a hint of congestion. On the ground there is order, an order imposed by an intricate web of paths, bridges, and elevated walkways that link its myriad private, public and commercial areas that manage, even in the shadows of its towering neighbors, to elicit a palpable village feel. Add to that a profusion of waterfalls, ponds, trees, streams, even structures entirely covered in vertical greenery and you have a rich architectural tapestry. There's a very real sense of community here, an integration of contemplative spaces that combines the soothing and much needed effects of nature with the conveniences of modern life.

Looking up, the white glass louvred exteriors of the towers are designed to make them appear to have been sculpted over millennia by the erosive effects of wind and water, giving them an organic feel that softens their imposing verticality. Designed in tandem with vertical shading fins they work together to add ventilation, filtered light and a calming feel to interior spaces. Like MAD projects elsewhere, there is a fusion here of architecture with the ancient Chinese landscape brush painting technique of *shan shui,* its buildings made to look as though they've been shaped over time rather than erected overnight.

Together the varied building blocks of this ground-breaking development combine to spell not alienation but harmony, and banishing any thoughts one might have of falling foul to futurist author Alvin Toffler's notion of 'Future Shock', his idea that 'too much change in too short a time' will have a dire psychological effects on us all. Far from alienating humanity, MAD's leap into the not-too-distant-future of metropolis-like developments should be a rallying call that the so-called 'shock of the new' need not be so shocking as it is . . . invigorating.

CHAPTER 12

Chaoyang Park Plaza

Beijing, China

MAD Architects

On the southern boundary of Beijing's central business district's largest park, a monumental project has recently been realized by Beijing-based MAD Architects. Chaoyang Park Plaza is a mixed-use development characterised by smooth, curved surfaces, a fusion of man and nature with stands of bamboo, native pines, water features and transplanted rocks mingling with two Armani-styled apartment buildings with protruding, staggered balconies, a variety of low-rise commercial buildings, and above it all the project's signature, towering statements – the assymetrical glazed twin towers that rise up like two emergent mountains, the centrepieces of MAD's extraordinary new urban canvas.

The 466 foot-high towers, connected by a glazed atrium, are a bold reflection of China's artistic heritage, more specifically the artists who popularized China's ancient landscape style of painting known as *shan shui,* a style of painting using brushes and ink and mostly depicting mountains. Coming to prominence in the 5th century, many of the principles of *shan shui* are seen here not just in its buildings, but also in the landscaping that surrounds them created by the great Japanese graphic artist Kanya Hara. In Chaoyang, Hara's pathways are never straight, but instead meander like a stream, mimicking nature's patterns, with each one leading you to a series of 'thresholds', places designed to welcome and envelop the walker.

Every example of *shan shui* must have a heart, a focal point, into which all of the other expressions converge. It must contain the meaning of the wider painting, in which will also be found the five elements of the natural world: water, earth, metal, fire and wood. At Chaoyang's heart is, of course, its stunning twin towers, adorned by *shan shui* motifs.

Shan shui uses snake-like, irregular lines to depict the country's mountainous northern regions, often layering one semi-concentric loop over the other, an approach that adds an illusion of depth in much the same way as do the tight, concentric lines one sees on a topographical map. Here, MAD took that ancient concept and adapted it to architecture, layering the façade of its towers with a series of increasingly precipitous

vaulted arches. The striking external fins on their glass façades also act as an efficient filtration and ventilation system.

With the gaze of visitors transfixed upon the twin tower's mesmerising organic forms it's possible to lose sight of the fact that there are actually ten buildings present here in this vast 22 hectare complex, each one strategically placed to form a series of open, yet at the same time secluded green spaces. MAD like to say that the smaller scale buildings are like small river pebbles when compared to the mountainous forms that loom over them, once large rocks that have been eroded and rounded with time.

MAD believe that Chinese architects need to move towards developing a truly Chinese style, that architects risk losing their independence if they become too involved

with commercial interests. Architects have the capacity to influence society, to provide practical responses to the challenge of climate change, to be more than mere designers. With Chaoyang Park Plaza, MAD have done something never attempted on this scale before: the marriage of modern architecture to the ancient art of *shan shui,* a world of black and white buildings meant to convey the same aesthetic resonance found in Chinese ink paintings. It's a marriage that's easily picked up on by Chinese visitors, but is an association western eyes have to be educated to appreciate in a development that sees itself not just as a collection of beautiful buildings, but as the culmination in architecture of hundreds of years of Chinese expressionism.

CENT
PARK
PLAZ
中央公园

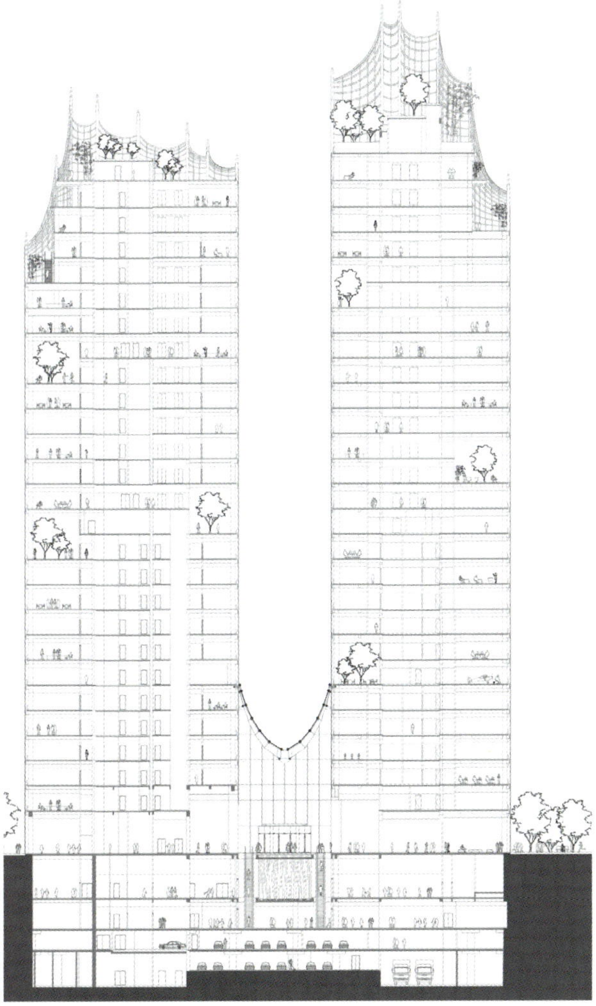

A5

A1
A2

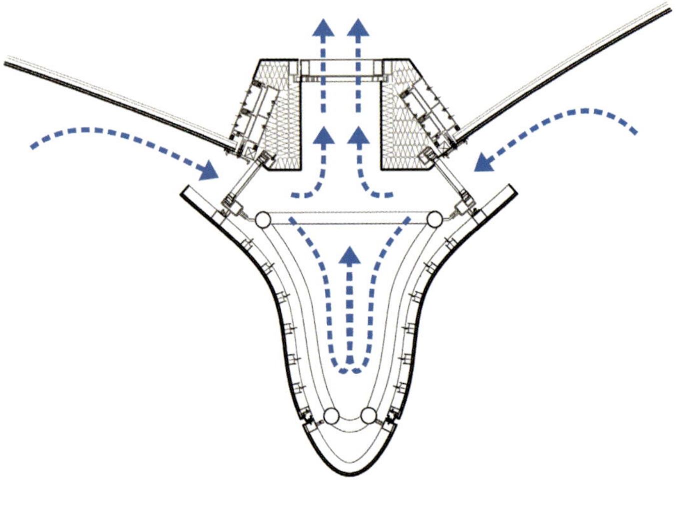

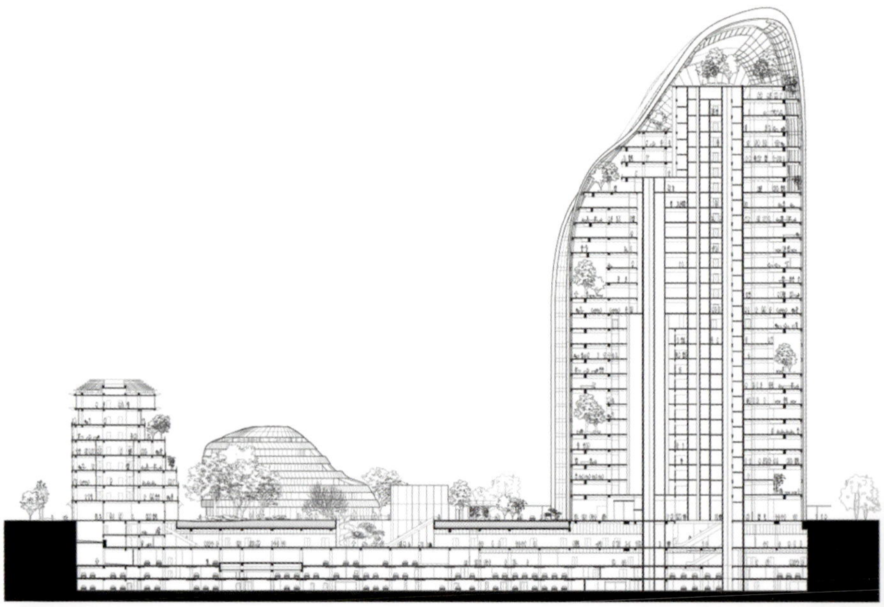

CHAPTER 13

V&A Dundee

Dundee, Scotland

Kengo Kuma & Associates

The construction process for any building is always a story in itself, but rarely more so than here in the radical, sculptural forms of V&A Dundee, Scotland's first design museum that has transformed the historic waterfront in the Scottish port city of Dundee. The building is without parallel and boasts a revolutionary design that would have been difficult to create even ten years ago because of the technology required to build it and the precision of its engineering. It is the first building in the United Kingdom to be designed by the great Japanese architect Kengo Kuma, whose design won out in an international field of 120 entries.

The Victoria & Albert (V&A) Dundee sits on a man-made peninsula on the northern banks of the Firth of Tay, a site made possible only after the construction of a temporary cofferdam (a watertight wall that allowed the draining of the river) before becoming a repository of more than 12,500 tonnes of rock, the building's weighty foundation. The dam, completed in May 2015, was the first hurdle in the museum's construction. The upper level was completed in October 2016, and the red and yellow formwork that had been enveloping it taken away in March 2017 (along with the cofferdam) finally giving the citizens of Dundee their first real glimpse at the building that would, in part, transform their city.

Next came the installation of almost 2500 cast stone panels, each poured in moulds and weighing as much as 3.3 tons, and individually secured to the structure's black concrete walls. The complexity of each unique piece required advanced 3D technology to ensure each would properly interlock with its neighbor. There's not one straight wall in any of the building's 21 external wall sections; not a single square foot of the façade that is the same as any other. Yet it manages to defy its massive concrete-filled volumes because its inverted shape gives it a smaller than expected footprint. It balances 'unpropped', yet despite its incongruous bulk is at home here. Why? Because like all good architecture it respects its environment. It looks like a moored ship: a centuries-old oaken hulk that has it fitting in nicely amongst the marine structures of the Dundee waterfront including the RRS *Discovery*, the famous barque-rigged Antarctic steamship

launched in 1901. And its extreme, inverted angles mimic the rugged granite cliffs that can be found along much of Scotland's eastern coastline.

At the heart of the museum is a wonderfully restored dark-stained oak tearoom created in 1908 by the great Scottish architect, artist and interior designer Charles Mackintosh (1868-1928), whose interest in Japanese aesthetics caught the eye of Kuma, who is a self-confessed admirer and who wanted to incorporate the tea room in his new museum. Created by Mackintosh when he was at the very pinnacle of his career for one of his most significant patrons who owned the tea rooms in Ingram Street, Glasgow, the double-height, 45 foot Oak Room was kept in storage in pieces for almost 50 years by Glasgow Museums, who rescued it from oblivion in 1971 when the building it was housed in was demolished.

All of its 1500 individual components – including all of its precious oak panels and stained glass details – were individually numbered. Plans were even drawn up detailing precisely how the room was built, with the hope one day it would be raised again. And one day it was, rebuilt in a room just large enough to house it, the 7000 sq foot workshop of Charles Taylor Woodwork in Dalkeith, south of Edinburgh.

The Mackintosh Tea Rooms are at the V&A Dundee on a 25-year loan, and the significance of its rebirth cannot be understated. It is unfurnished, and lit with the very same electric lights Mackintosh originally intended it to have. Now a walk-through exhibit, the room is 95 percent original, and to immerse yourself in it is, quite simply, a privilege. It is one of Scotland's most irreplaceable interiors.

There is also much about this building that one cannot see, like the 30 x 656 ft deep

bore holes that were drilled into the earth below, which provide it with its geothermal heating – a bravura example of environmental engineering taken after a Low and Zero Carbon Technologies study was undertaken to determine which form of renewable energy would best suit its design. Supplemented by roof-mounted air sourced heat pumps, more than 800,000 kWh of heating and 500,000 kWh of cooling is generated onsite annually.

The first branch of London's Victoria & Albert Museum, V&A Dundee has taken hold of an old port area, once a bustling centre of the now defunct jute industry (vegetable fibres capable of being spun into strong, coarse threads) which has long since lost its relevance and been a barrier between the city and the water, and given it new life. The latest manifestation in a worldwide trend to turn decrepit waterfronts into energetic new centres of urbanity and refinement, V&A Dundee represents just one

piece in a larger social transformation that will be ongoing for the next three decades. It is hoped that buildings proposed to rise up in its vicinity will not hem it in.

In January 2019 the respected London-based international design magazine *Wallpaper* named V&A Dundee the world's best new public building. But of course it is much more than a building. It is, ironically, both 'superstructure' – an 86,100 sq ft building with 17,760 sq ft of gallery space – and 'meeting place', what Kengo Kuma refers to as 'a living room for the city'. The hope amongst Dundonians who are tired of Dundee being viewed in Scotland as Glasgow's 'poor relative' and seen as just an industrial hub struggling with economic decline, is that Kuma's masterpiece will reinvigorate their city and be seen as it should be – as a living room that the whole world will want to come and see.

V&A

V&A

CHAPTER 14

Tirpitz Museum

Blåvand, Denmark

Bjarke Ingels Group (BIG)

In August 1944 outside the small coastal village of Blåvand on the west coast of Denmark's Jutland Peninsula, occupying Nazi forces were building a 7500 sq ft concrete bunker complex that would never be finished, one of some 200 bunkers that had been raised along the Danish coast. Known as the Tirpitz Bunker after the great German battleship of the same name, it was a part of Adolf Hitler's Atlantic Wall, an ambitious but ultimately futile defensive line designed to thwart the Allied landings in Europe that the German High Command knew were coming. The bunker's gun emplacement was designed to house a massive 15 inch gun that had been recovered from a decommissioned battleship. But it was never installed. The war came to an end, and the site was abandoned.

In 1991 the local municipality converted the space into a small museum which told visitors the story of the Atlantic Wall. In 2012 a decision was taken to enlarge the museum and create four new gallery spaces. It would be a monumental conversion of a challenging, restrictive site, and Bjarke Ingels Group (BIG) were commissioned to bring it to fruition.

BIG's approach was complicated not only because of the nature of the existing building, but also because it was sited within a nature preserve which prevented any outward construction. Then it was realised one of the dunes wasn't in fact natural, but instead was the remains of a berm, a man-made terrace or raised embankment built to support the train tracks that would one day carry wagons laden with shells from the port to the bunker. This allowed for some altering of the terrain and the creation of pathways. Shortlisted in the 'Culture – Completed Buildings' category at the 2018 World Architecture Festival, the Tirpitz Museum is a triumph of integration, with its new glazed surfaces bringing in light where it can, and the surrounding pathways set in the midst of heath and other coastal flora. In the distance there are fields alive with poppies.

The four ramp-like cuts originally made into the surrounding sandy terrain to access the bunker are still the museum's entry points. Slender and imbued with a dramatic feel that increases anticipation for what lies ahead, they take you first into its central courtyard and from there down into the bunker's sunken, concrete-walled void. Lit in part by a series of soaring 20 foot-high glass panels, the complex now comprises four gallery spaces, each of which can be accessed independently from the courtyard, or one after the next via a continuous internal loop.

The galleries each tell their own stories. *An Army of Concrete* is devoted to the story of the Atlantic Wall and contains a series of small rooms each of which share the story of someone who lived in the area during the dark days of the war. People such as Alice, whose family had to leave their home so that it could be turned into accommodation for German soldiers. *The Gateway to the West* concentrates on local history. *The Gold of the West Coast* houses Denmark's largest collection of amber – the 'gold of the ocean'– complete with gorgeous recreations of 35 million year-old trees that are literally dripping with the golden resin. The fourth gallery is reserved for special exhibitions.

It's ironic that a massed volume like this should exist in the midst of such a fragile landscape. Yet BIG have exceeded their brief. What was once a heavy, rusting, monolithic form has been transformed into an open, inviting space. Cantilevered roofs of rough, cast-in-situ concrete designed by the Swiss structural engineering firm of Lüchinger+Meyer support the courtyard's 20 foot-high windows. And while building restrictions may have hindered the modernizing of its external appearance, inside adjustable floor planes, moveable walls and a series of intersecting staircases have combined to create a powerful, if not disorienting architectural statement.

TIRPITZ

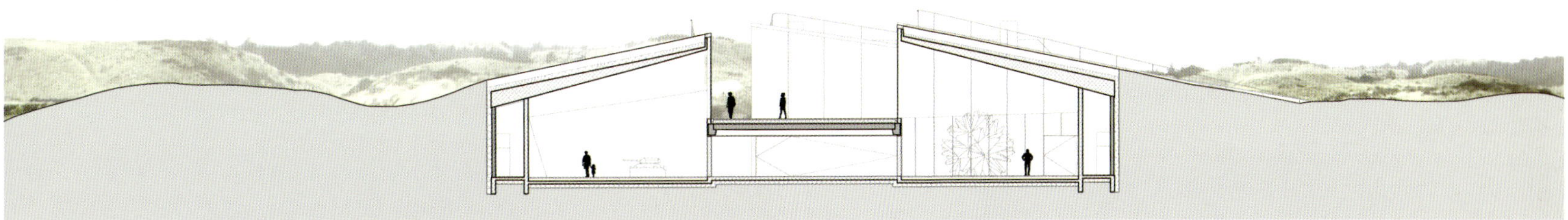

TIRPITZ

SFMOMA

CHAPTER 15

San Francisco Museum of Modern Art (SFMOMA)

San Francisco, California, USA

Mario Botta and Snøhetta

The first incarnation of the San Francisco Museum of Modern Art was designed by Mario Botta, the Swiss-born architect and former pupil of Le Corbusier. It opened to the public in 1995 and, despite being received coolly by critics at the time, came to be regarded as a triumph of monumental, postmodern architecture. Botta's design, chosen over competing entries from Tadao Ando and Frank Gehry, was at the time the largest building in the American West dedicated to the arts. It would also carry the burden of attempting to single-handedly spark the revitalization of a somewhat dilapidated area of the city – the then blighted neighborhood of SoMa (to the South of Market Street).

Botta was a little old fashioned, preferring to work with masonry rather than glass or steel, which made him, as a somewhat reluctant Postmodernist, difficult to categorize. His five-story layered composition of stacked boxes, with its orthogonal volumes and red brick exterior, was constructed using a variety of very 'unmodern' materials such as stone and wood, which combined to give it a heavy appearance. And of course there was that signature rooftop 'turret' with its enigmatic banded black and white stones, sliced off at an angle which made the whole thing just impossible to ignore. Botta always spoke of the turret and its glass roof – his 'oculus' – as the building's great eye, providing a connection between its rather cavernous interior and the outside world, a looking glass from within, an intriguing portal from without. A brooding Cyclops of brick and mortar.

Yet despite its impressive size, in recent years the problem of available space came to bedevil SFMOMA in much the same way as it has museums worldwide where public art has a penchant for increasing in size with every new installation. Add to that the announcement of a new partnership with the renowned Doris and Donald Fisher Collection of postwar and contemporary art – a total of over 1100 works by 185 artists – and it became clear that something had to be done. The museum needed to grow. Enter: Snøhetta.

In 2009 the museum announced plans for a major expansion, and in 2010 a campaign was announced by museum and community leaders to select an architectural firm who could help SFMOMA realize its lofty ambitions. The Oslo-based firm Snøhetta was selected, and from 2013 to 2016 the museum was closed to the public. Purpose-built to house the museum's new acquisitions, Snøhetta integrated a 10-story expansion into Botta's existing work and in the process expanded the museum's gallery space three-fold adding almost 172,220 sq ft of outdoor and indoor galleries, as well as increased public spaces, educational and performance spaces, conservation rooms, and an enlarged museum store and restaurant.

Such fundamental changes were only made possible by directing the expansion up and behind the existing building, an addition that stretched the entire length of the city block from Minna Street to Howard Street, and on the way opening up new entrances off of mid-block streets. In a further attempt to integrate the building and engage passers-by a series of external windows at street level have been installed to allow

pedestrians a peek inside into various gallery spaces in the hope of drawing them in. Snøhetta was so determined to create an interplay between the museum's interior and the city beyond that the window mullions on the ground floor were made out of plate steel rather than traditional aluminium, torch-cut into impossibly thin, stick-like joints to maximize the amount of natural light the gallery received and eliminate as much as possible any sense of separation.

You can come into its public spaces, feel a part of the museum, and, if you don't want to, you don't have to enter the galleries or pay for a ticket. 'We wanted to open the door to people who have little knowledge of modern art', wrote Craig Dykers, a Snøhetta founder, 'and provide refinement and focus for longtime art enthusiasts'. As if to trumpet the museum's new open door policy, the maple-faced Roman steps in the Roberts Family Gallery has lost little time in becoming one of the city's most desirable new meeting places.

Still inside, a new sculptural staircase replaces Botta's original stairway (which blocked some of the light streaming down from the oculus) and takes visitors up to the second floor from its base in the Evelyn and Walter Haas Jr. Atrium. Outside, the largest 'living wall' in the United States, three stories high and half a city block long is filled with more than 19,000 plants over three levels, 21 species of which are endemic to California; an ever-changing artwork kept alive by a purpose-built watering system where pH and moisture levels are monitored by hidden sensors.

The museum's new external façade, inspired by the city's famous fogs and the waters of San Francisco Bay consists of over 700 fibreglass reinforced polymers (FRP's), panels that have been attached to a curtain-wall to create a visual feast: vast expanses of rippling, horizontal bands, their angular appearance and composition (they are embedded with particles of local sand) giving the impression they move with the changing light, mimicking the ripples of the water in the city's famous bay. Lighter than steel and cheaper than concrete the lines of the façade were carefully crafted to echo Botta's original brickwork, its whiteness a nuanced reflection of the turret's white granite. Rarely used up to that point on buildings more than four stories tall, its choice as a cladding was groundbreaking, its flowing form a juxtaposition to Botta's bricks that Snøhetta likened to a dance: be too much like your partner and you risk stomping on each other's feet. But be a little different, possess your own personality, your own distinct rhythm, and the two of you will co-exist in perfect harmony.

And as is often the case with truly great buildings, there are the little things that can so easily be overlooked – like the absence of floor vents. Museums dislike floor vents but need them to help maintain a stable temperature. In SFMOMA, Snøhetta first shrunk the duct outlets then decided instead to put them in the ceiling, streamlining its floors. Its LED's can dim in tiny 1 percent increments, then diffuse the light by bouncing if off overhead reflectors. And to reduce 'acoustic flutter' – the noise we all make when we're in a confined area – ceilings have been coated with a special sound-dampening plaster imbued with glass beads, while the wood in its staircases was scoured with cuts and grooves: graveyards where sound waves go to die.

Rarely has a building had an interior and exterior so radically and thoughtfully transformed, with vast new spaces inside and something akin to a tabular iceberg now firmly hemmed in along Third Street, growing out of Botta's stoic ziggurat.

CHAPTER 16

Zhang Zhidong & Modern Industrial Museum

Wuhan, China

Studio Libeskind

Zhang Zhidong was born in Guizhou Province, China, in 1837 during the late Qing dynasty to a family of scholar/officials. A confident, precocious student always destined for a life in the civil service, he passed its entrance exam at the age of 13 with ease, and went on to become one of the foremost officials and reformers of his time. Deeply committed to China's social and economic renewal, he established processes to better educate its bureaucrats; arranged for students to study abroad; restructured China's school system and greatly expanded the number of schools and institutes of learning; and initiated the translation of Western and Japanese-authored books. Zhang Zhidong also was a fundamental figure in modernizing China's heavy industry, including the modernization of the city of Wuhan and the establishment of its vital steel industry. So it is appropriate that a museum should at last be raised to honor Zhang Zhidong's lifetime of service, and the early stirrings of Chinese industrialism.

... and where better to build it than alongside Wuhan's old steelworks?

At once a monument to Wuhan's industrial past and a beacon pointing the way to a new and exciting future, the arching, steel-clad volumes of the Zhang Zhidong Museum seemingly defy gravity; its exhibition spaces arcing their way upwards in a symbolic display of confidence, momentum and modernity.

The first Chinese project by world-renowned Polish-American architect Daniel Libeskind, the museum has three levels, each with its own dedicated brief. While the entrance, main stairway, administrative offices, library and museum shop are all housed within its two conventional steel and glass structures, its upper levels are given over to the life of Zhang Zhidong, an overview of the nation's steel and iron industry, and the rich industrial heritage of the city of Wuhan. All the museum's levels are connected by a single, central atrium that brings in an abundance of natural light to a series of exhibits which have been finely tuned by exhibition designers Diameter Narrative Design. The exhibits ably show off the industrial prowess and innovation brought to China by Zhang

Zhidong at the dawn of the 20th Century, and how they still have relevance today.

The second floor contains the sort of internal geometric forms long favored by Libeskind, and includes a semi-circular auditorium beneath an oculus – a round, eye-like aperture that looks out over the ageing steelworks. At the building's apex a striking latticed opening provides expansive views over the city and down onto the nautical-themed geometric lines, rings and newly-planted gardens in the plaza below which serves to connect the building to the city. 'By lifting the museum up', Libeskind explained, 'we were able to create a new public plaza while delivering to the city a world-class cultural institution that reflects the future and spirit of Wuhan'.

The building's signature architectural motif is its glorious, sweeping prow, its nod to the uplifted bow of a ship and homage to the vessels that have long ploughed the waters of the nearby Yangtze River. Sheathed in triangular steel panels the uplifted arc, or as Liebeskind himself prefers to describe it, his 'horizontal shard' is supported by the two adjacent glass towers. It is a sight to behold from street level, but from inside the shard itself perhaps even more so, with the two walls of its arced exterior causing the floor to gradually disappear in a 'vanishing point', the apparent convergence of two parallel lines, that aren't really there, but can be if you look hard enough. Libeskind enjoys playing with illusions, creating angular spaces that can potentially disorient the viewer. One only has to look at his Jewish Museum in Berlin with its alternating, maze-like spatial layouts. You can feel its echoes here.

Building in China for the first time presented a new set of challenges for Liebeskind. Working in the offices of local architect Zhong Nan Design a mock-up model was constructed, itself a novel approach to design in China, and ways were sought to simplify the design to fit with local technologies. And there were all of the usual problems of communication, and not just words but sharing the intent and vision and making sure it all translated into the end product everyone was hoping for.

And in the end, it did. More than 3500 tons of steel went into its construction, at once a homage to Wuhan's past and a statement of confidence in its future. The suburban intersection of Qintai and Jiangcheng Avenues, the former site of the Zhang Zhidong & Hanyang Ironworks Museum will never look the same again. Even so, two of the museum's most precious exhibits are the original boundary stone and memorial tablet of the old Hanyang Ironworks, China's earliest ironworks. The 120 year-old boundary stone was found at, of all places, the nearby Qingchuan Hotel, where it was being used in ignorance as a stepping stone. The square memorial tablet, located in 2012, has on it the inscription 'Luxembourg', evidence of that country's involvement in the engineering of the original Hanyang Ironworks, which opened for the first time in 1894.

The emergence of the first ironworks in China (and indeed in Asia) was no small thing, and Liebeskind's soaring testament to China's nascent industrialism provides a vibrant new space for its continued study and appreciation.

历史学家看张之洞
INSIGHTS FROM HISTORIANS

CHAPTER 17

007 ELEMENTS

Sölden, Austria

Obermoser arch-omo ZT GmbH

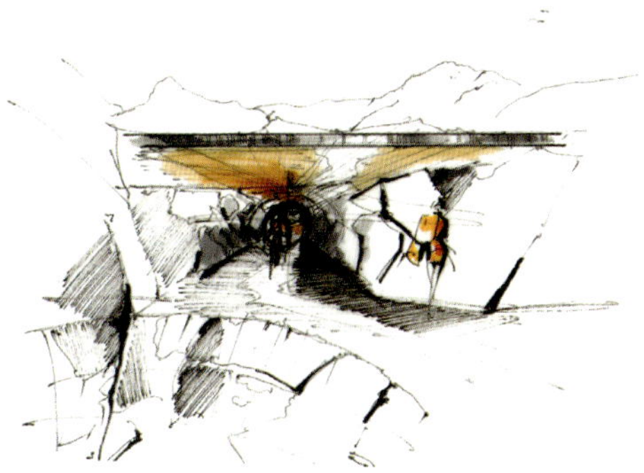

It sits at 9974 feet above sea level, inside the summit of Gaislachkogl Mountain in Sölden, Austria: a concrete hideaway that would be the envy of any Bond villain. Accessed via a high-speed cable car, 007 Elements by the Innsbruck-based architect Johann Obermoser is part museum, part interactive installation, and part mountaintop lair.

Inside you'll encounter nine separate galleries designed to provide you with the 007 Elements 'Experience'. Designed by Tino Schaedler at the creative agency Optimist Inc. and Neal Callow, the *James Bond* Art Director on the last four Bond films, each gallery showcases an 'element' that is characteristic of a Bond film in a homage to the Bond legacy though with a special emphasis on *Spectre*, the fourth film starring the current 007, Daniel Craig. As visitors progress through each gallery they are taken on a journey through the senses courtesy of a phalanx of lights, shadows, visual projections and disorienting soundscapes and perspectives that combine to deliver an immersive, theatrical experience. Every gallery is connected by ramps that take you in an imperceptibly downward direction, which has you exiting the mountain 30 feet below where you entered. On a mountaintop where cable cars continually bring in a fair amount of piste ski traffic, ramps are preferable to stairs.

To come here is to find yourself in a classic Bond-like landscape. Not only are you on an isolated, snow-covered European summit overlooking the Ötztal Alps, you're also right next to the iCE-Q Restaurant, which doubled as the Hoffler Klinik in *Spectre*. Almost the entire museum is buried within the mountain with only its entry and exit, a small viewing area and two large panoramic windows projecting beyond its rocky exterior. Concrete, steel and glass are used throughout, giving the interior an austere though very Bond-like appearance. Galleries are divided by black stainless-steel doors, black perforated steel panels hang from the ceilings and act as sound dampeners, while beautiful volumes of angled case-concrete provide imposing spatial vistas.

Each gallery is unique. The Tech Lab is filled with Q-like gadgets, The Lair contains 360 degree visuals depicting scenes from classic Bond movies, while the Action Hall

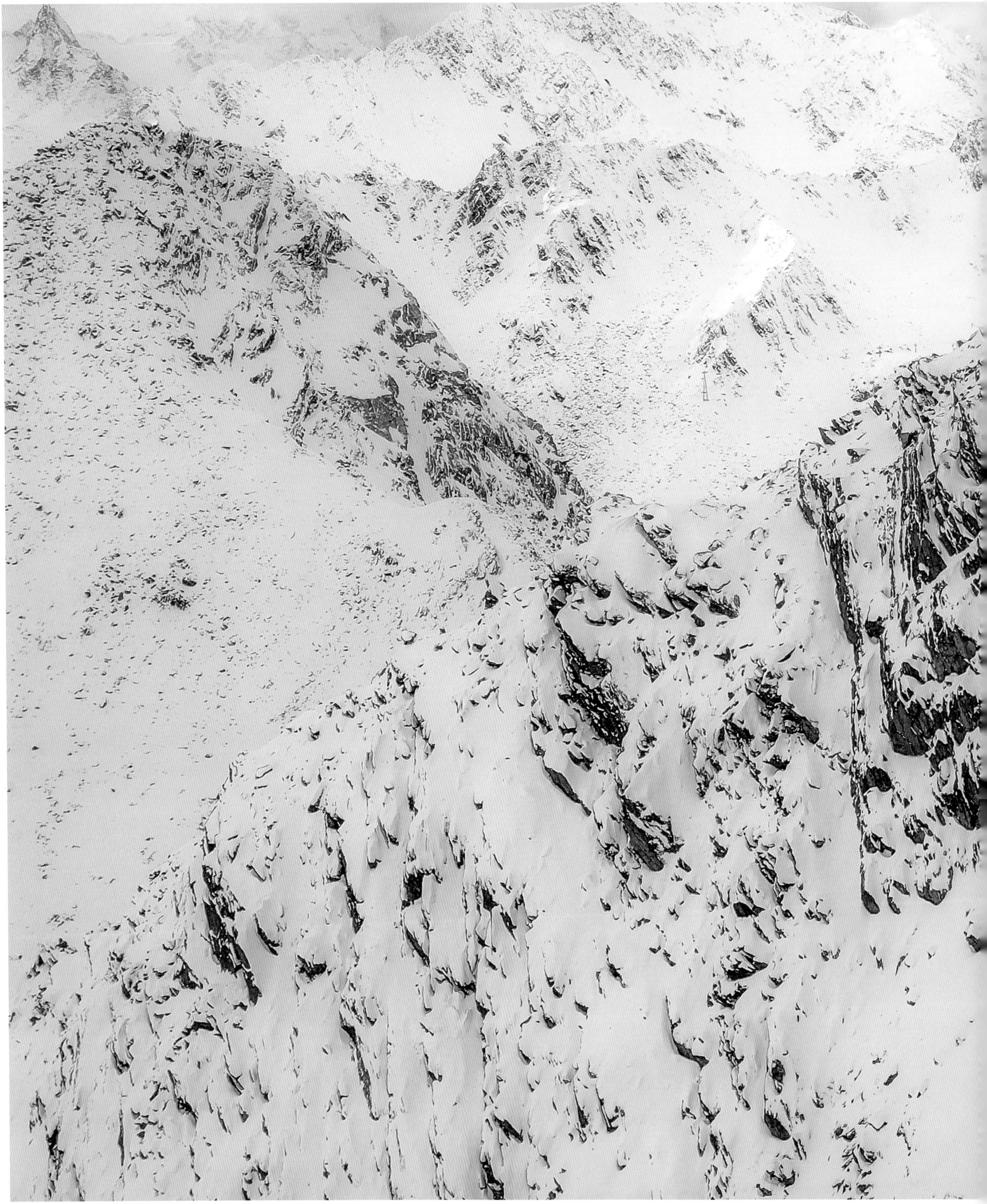

has a full-size suspended mock-up of the Britten-Norman airplane Bond flew in *Spectre's* gripping snow-chase scene with all those pursuing Land Rovers, complete with shards of glass all about it providing a visceral sense of motion as though it's crashing in real time right through the museum's plate glass windows.

The decision not to include any form of heating or air-conditioning within the building was taken early on in the design stage, it's 1 degree Celsius internal temperature maintained thanks to a series of voids between its internal and external walls, helping visitors to better appreciate the extreme nature of its location while reducing its impact upon the permafrost over which it sits.

Obermoser found inspiration for 007 Elements in the sets of the late Sir Kenneth Adam, the set designer on seven Bond films in the 1960s and 70s, from *Dr. No* in 1962 to *Moonraker* in 1979. It is a wonderfully bespoke brutalist structure, realised thanks to the 10 million Euro budget given to it by its owner Jakob Falkner, and given to Obermoser because Falkner was already familiar with the adjacent iCE-Q Restaurant, also an Obermoser project. Early conceptual discussions toyed with the idea of creating a dish-shaped structure here, angled like a satellite receiver 45 degrees towards the heavens but which was too problematic given the constraints of the site. Finally came the 'villainous' solution: a hidden lair, echoing the 'iceberg principle' as Obermoser prefers to call it: What you see from afar is merely a tantalising tease when compared to what lies beneath.

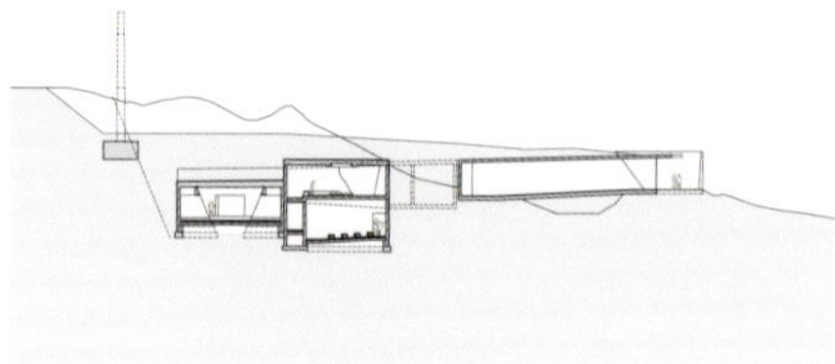

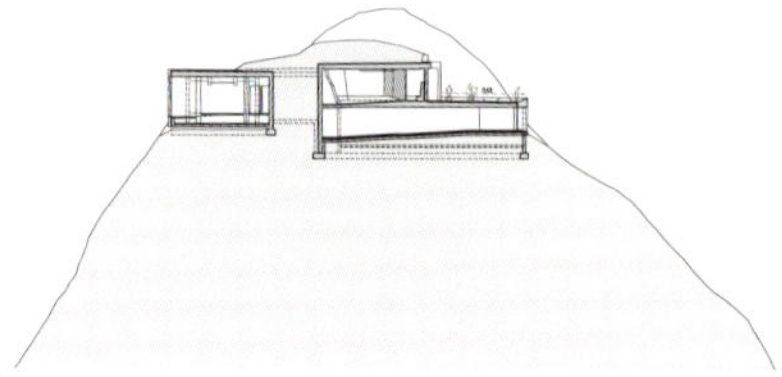

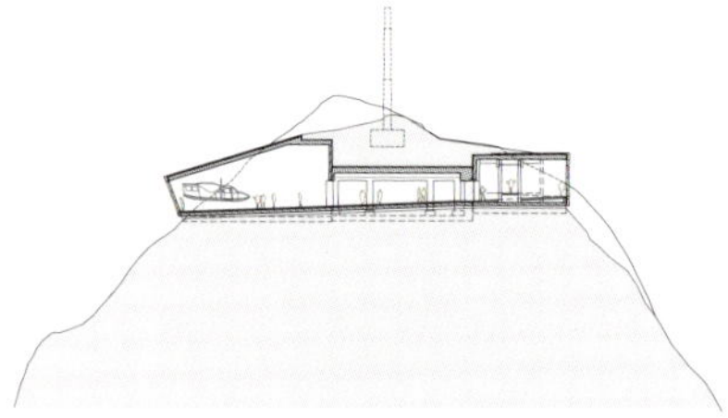

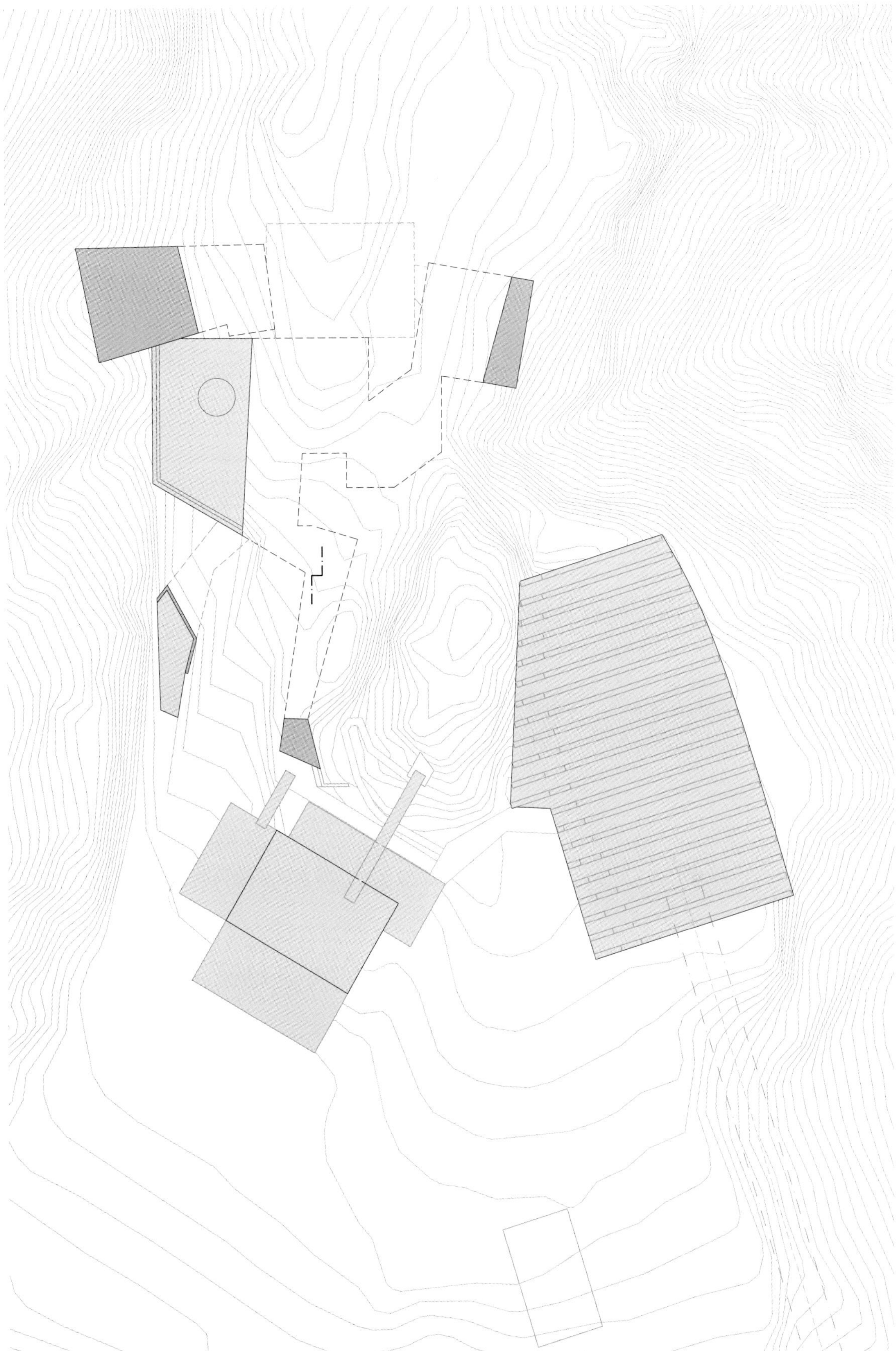

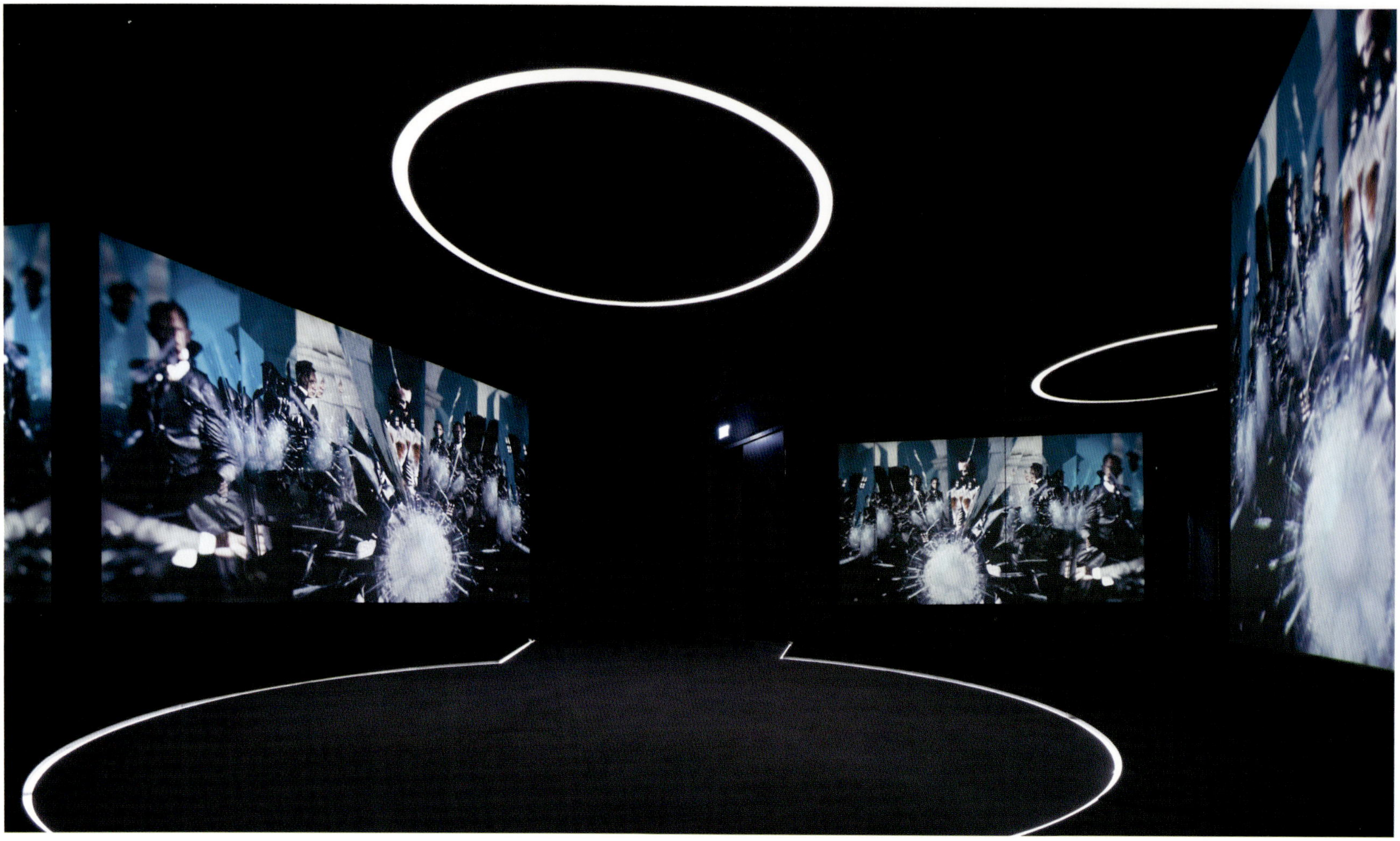

LÉA SEYDOUX
MADELEINE SWANN SPECTRE 2015
DANIEL CRAIG
JAMES BOND SPECTRE 2015

ELEMENTS

CHAPTER 18

Fondation Louis Vuitton

Paris, France

Gehry Partners

When architect Frank Gehry first visited the proposed site of what would one day become the Fondation Louis Vuitton, located in the Bois de Boulogne on the western edge of the 16th arrondissement in Paris, tears filled his eyes. The site was a powerful one, the land having been ceded to the city by Emperor Napoleon III in 1852 so it could be turned into a public park. It was also where one of his favorite French novelists, Marcel Proust, played as a child. But the site came with restrictions. Local building codes meant nothing solid over two stories could be raised, and Gehry's vision extended well beyond that constricting set of boundaries. Fortunately, though, glass was not deemed to be a solid material. And so Gehry began to exploit his 'glass loophole'.

The Fondation Louis Vuitton met its height restriction despite rising some 164 feet into the air, and was a dozen years in the making. It was financed by the wealthiest man in France, business magnate and ardent art enthusiast Bernard Arnault who wanted a world-class venue to showcase his own burgeoning art collection. When Gehry and Arnault first sat down and Gehry showed him some of his initial sketches for the proposed building, Arnault chose the most complex, the most chaotic of them all. Gehry was excited by his client's enthusiasm and vision; what evolved was in many ways born of the spirit of Arnault's conviction and the resultant dialogue he and the architect began to have. Had Arnault not chosen the sketch he had, what would have evolved would have been very different to the building we can now all enjoy.

What rose up here in the Bois de Boulogne was a typical Gehry-like structure, its exterior gloriously fragmented and with no actual façade, with two stories of gallery space above ground and one dug, grotto-like, from the earth beneath – all of it topped by a pavilion consisting of twelve extraordinary shell-shaped glass panels. 'The idea of using glass,' Gehry told *Architectural Digest*, 'was a positive force in gaining support from the mayor of Paris. And it was essential in making the Fondation a true Bois de Boulogne building, in the spirit of a children's park'.

The lower galleries are set below ground level in a watery world of reflecting pools and cascading waterfalls, all wrapped in a white-walled central tower that Gehry and

those at Gehry Partners liked to call the 'Iceberg'. The Iceberg, clad in fibre-reinforced concrete, contains all the museum's very classical gallery spaces – 11 in total – as well as traditional viewing areas specifically requested by the museum's curator and a 350-seat auditorium. Above it all, set on sinewy-looking supports of wood and steel, are the sails: a soaring world of glass which was developed independently from the building below then brought to site and integrated to form a singular expression of radical modernism, a symbiosis of form, function, and that unmistakable Gehry style.

Unconcerned with how it would look from above, the building was designed to create a relationship with the viewer as they approached it at ground level, walking across the park lands of the Bois de Boulogne, its glass sails projecting above the treetops, a floating ship in a sea of green. And while the orthogonal spaces of the galleries may be very gallery-like, the torquing apertures in their ceilings are anything but orthodox: gorgeous sculptural elements that filter in light from above. (Originally the design called for 14 glass sails, but cost overruns saw the number reduced to twelve).

The introduction of wood into the supports gave the interior a much less sterile appearance. A complex array of over-engineered, zig-zagging, glue-laminated braces, brackets and struts reach high into its roof terraces, their complexity requiring the creation of no less than 30 technical patents, all for a space that was purposefully left to look unfinished so that people – both children and adults- could be invited by the museum to play with the spaces between the sails and the buildings, fill them with their own artworks, their own inner expressions.

The glass shells are more than mere ornaments. They take us back in time, Gehry once said: way, way back – 300, maybe 400 million years – to our beginnings in the sea.

We came from the ocean, the architect believes, which is why his buildings so often are fish-like, shell-like, imbued with marine symbolism. Note his Golden Fish Sculpture El Peix on the Barcelona waterfront. These shells on the Fondation Louis Vuitton speak to us because they evoke our rise as a species. The building was meant to facilitate our creative consciousness, to encourage us to experiment with what it means to be human. 'I have given you a violin', Gehry told the museum's creator. 'Now you've got to play it'.

The building set new standards in the use of groundbreaking digital design and construction methods. A web-hosted 3D digital model allowed for the simultaneous input of engineering maxims, design models and assembly guidelines from over 400 engineers and designers – an approach that resulted in world-first applications of fabrication technologies. Industrial robotics were programmed with advanced mathematical formulas to simulate the placement of more than 19,000 concrete panels and 3600 glass panels.

Most buildings are static things, but the Fondation Louis Vuitton seems to move, its shells filled with air, propelling it, giving it energy. And they provide a playful air, too: a marine-like form that calls out to the children at play in the amusement park and green spaces of the neighboring Jardin d'Acclimatation. 'Come over here', it seems to say. 'You can play here, too'.

Gehry has admitted to really 'feeling' this building, and surely that is what great architecture is meant to do – elicit feelings. Architecture can, when done properly, be an act of social conscience. A building can make people feel loved, feel accepted, provide them with shelter, and make spirits soar. The Fondation Louis Vuitton does all this and more in a building that lifts architecture into the lofty realm of art.

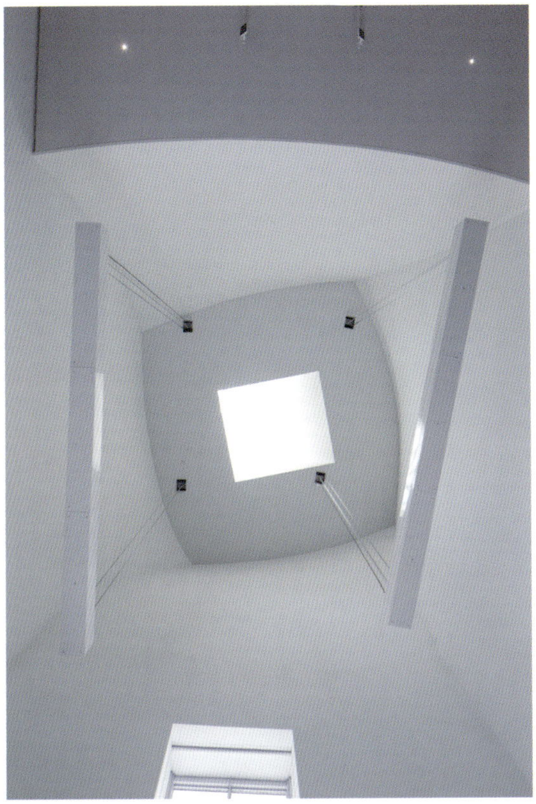

BOX
MSK

CHAPTER 19

Nike Box MSK

Moscow, Russian Federation

Kosmos Architects & Strelka KB

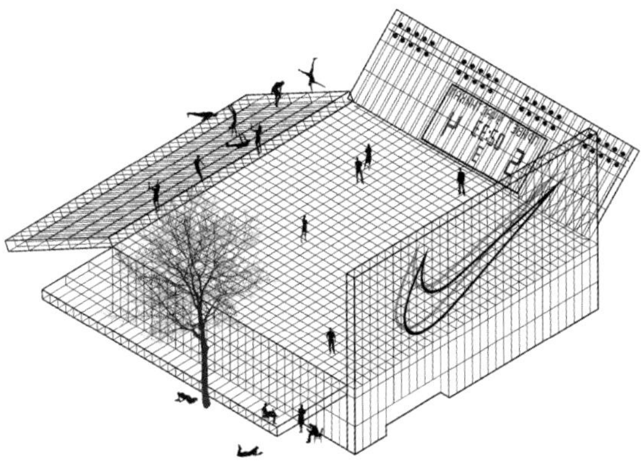

Moscow's Gorky Park was named after Maxim Gorky, the Russian writer and founder of 1930s 'socialist realism', the idealised depiction in literature of communism's core values, such as the emancipation of the working class. In keeping with Gorky's notion of advancing the Soviet state, Gorky Park was always as much an exhibition space for the state's industrial achievements as it was a green world into which Muscovites could retreat to gain respite from what has always been an overly urban city. Despite a rise in the country's environmental movement in recent years and numerous efforts to add greenery to Moscow's grey urbanity, the park still remains a showcase for technical innovation. But there are some pretty impressive architectural statements here nowadays, including OMA's Garage Museum of Contemporary Art. But the sought after blurring of nature with architecture is nowhere seen to better effect than in the park's most exciting new addition, Nike Box MSK.

Designed by Moscow-based architectural firm Kosmos Architects in cooperation with Strelka KB, Nike Box MSK reflects the values and lifestyle of modern Muscovites, inspired in part by Russia's prefabricated apartment blocks called *korobki* (boxes) – outdoor areas enclosed by protective fences, the sort of places that can be found on the periphery of many a Russian city. The 1815 square mile site, with its nearby industrial architecture and rugged neighborhoods, is open year round, providing free access to all of its facilities which include an outdoor football field and three-on-three basketball courts, indoor and outdoor spaces for training and yoga, and is also the clubhouse for Moscow's Nike Running Club.

The building is defined by five primary design principles: transparency, openness, the manipulation of the site, how it integrates itself into the surrounding parkland, and how it provides inspiration for the pursuit of sport, health and wellness. Its naked external frame provides the building its transparent façade and open plan, helping to integrate it in the surrounding greenery and revealing its interior to the street. It's inclined 'flaps' allow people to use its rooftop, while its strikingly vivid magenta landscape of red supportive rubber provide its interiors with energy and inspiration.

The three dimensional façade is a metal lattice that acts as a membrane between its interior and the park, allowing in air and light. The openness of the framework allows trees to grow through the building, and on sun-filled days the building's flaps give protection and provide its surrounds with ornamental shadows that continually shift with the sun. Nike Box MSK's rooftop is also useful, maximizing the space available for public activity and designed to be a platform for everything from yoga classes and public announcements to parties as well as art and cultural exhibits.

The building's square footprint is divided into four distinct parts: entry hall, multi-purpose hall, dressing rooms and a utility block, which are bisected by two intersecting corridors. Moveable partitions can open up the entrance hall and multi-purpose hall into a single larger space. From above it all looks a bit like an open shoebox, Nike's signature image.

The transformation of Gorky Park and the construction of buildings like Nike Box MSK typifies Russia's breaking free of the austere post World War II brutalism that came to characterise its cities. The country's blight of towering box-like apartment complexes with little or no green and recreational spaces to accompany them has caused a rift in the fabric of life throughout the country, a rift that is only beginning to be addressed by architects like those at Kosmos and Strelka who see cities not as rationalist impersonal spaces numb to the needs of their inhabitants, but as integrated, living organisms, enriching our sense of community and purpose.

BOX
MSK

양천향교
강서로
공항
마곡동로
N
S
Magokdong-ro

CHAPTER 20

Kolon One & Only Tower

Seoul, South Korea

Morphosis Architects

The Kolon One & Only Tower in the South Korean capital of Seoul is the new headquarters and research and development hub for the South Korean firm Kolon Industries. It was founded in 1957 as Korea Nylon Incorporated., one of a handful of family-owned businesses that prospered in the wake of World War II and helped transform the country into an economic giant. Kolon had specialized for years in the design and manufacturing of electronic components, chemicals and industrial materials, even high-grade technical hiking apparel. Kolon is also known for the fabricating of a range of cutting-edge textiles – a level of knowledge and expertise which, when combined with the imaginative flair of the designers and engineers at Morphosis Architects has resulted in the creation of one of the country's most striking commercial structures, and taken the idea of 'polymers' and their potential into a new and hitherto unheard of aesthetic realm.

Morphosis were asked to create a building that would maximize the available sunlight, while at the same time minimize heat gain. The solution? Use Kolon's own fabrics to make hundreds of diamond-shaped linear panels, nicknamed 'stretchers', in a variety of thicknesses and translucency, and install them vertically inside the building's 100 foot-tall atrium to diffuse the powerful afternoon sun. The stretchers not only help with the sun but are also a powerful acoustic tool, and when the light becomes too diffused, a series of well-placed LED's can provide the required illumination.

A total of ten different Kolon-manufactured fabrics are used throughout the building's internal and external spaces and, as clever as its interior is, it is Kolon One & Only's exterior that makes it simply impossible to ignore, clad, jacket-like, in hundreds of polymer panels, specially tiered to maximize shade and to work in tandem with the stretchers inside to minimize heat gain. The material chosen as an adjunt to the glass-fibre reinforced polymers – aramid – is a heat-resistant synthetic fibre used as ballistic armor in the military and aerospace industries, with five times the tensile strength of iron. The panel's strength allowed for the panels to be installed using relatively few connection points, maximising external views from inside the building. The presence of aramid also meant the panels would easily contend with the region's fierce winds and extreme temperature fluctuations.

Located in the southwest Seoul suburb of Magok, an area the local government is redefining as a tech-heavy mini-city, Kolon One & Only's unapologetic, futuristic 820,200 square feet is spread over its 5 acre site, the building a synthesis of two distinct volumes. The more dramatic of the two – its wonderfully folded, polymer-clad exoskeleton not unlike some woven metallic fabric – looks out towards the emerging neighborhood's central park, all of it resting on its primary supports: a series of carbon fibre reinforced concrete piers that rise up in an impressive array of obtuse and acute angles.

The 328,000 ft-long atrium, wrapped in its curvaceous, polymer skin, is a whopping 130 feet high and doubles as the building's primary social hub. A grand, monumental staircase that took its inspiration from Rome's 18th Century Spanish Steps takes workers to the offices above and, like its historic counterpart has been designed to cater for informal staircase gatherings. Natural light is everywhere here, which reduces the building's need for artificial lighting, and there's a green space and an array of photovoltaic panels on its roof, an approach to energy use and air quality that has earned Kolon One & Only Leadership in Energy and Environmental Design (LEED) certification.

But not every environmental innovation in Kolon One & Only is so easy to spot. Well aware that around 5 percent of the planet's CO_2 emissions are estimated to be a by-product of the extraction and production of cement, Kolon and Morphosis decided the concrete in its foundations and floors would contain an innovative new approach to sustainable construction: Bubble Deck. Bubble Deck's precast concrete slabs contain large, hollow plastic balls, held in place inside prefabricated wire restraints. Its biaxial technology means concrete floors can be thinner, while retaining the performance of reinforced concrete. The 'voids' inside the yellow balls also creates a lattice effect that reduces the weight of a slab by 35 percent and the amount of actual concrete required by over 30 percent Floors are laid faster, and construction and transportation costs are reduced.

The three laboratory wings are housed within the folded volume, set within a building which took more than five years to design and construct and is now the centre of the company's research and development. Kolon One & Only also perfectly reflects the sort of non-traditional, hyper-engineered forms so beloved by Morphosis Architect's founder, Thom Mayne.

In the end, though, it is the drama-filled inflection of its western façade, and the hundreds of shark tooth-like panels that shroud it that defines this wonderful building. Sure, its three other elevations certainly complete the holistic design and allow Kolon's 38 R&D divisions to effectively communicate with one another to help the company maximize its own resources and achievements. But the fabulously arching façade is without doubt the architectural tour de force here, filled with laboratories, conference rooms and public spaces on the inside, it perfectly embodies Kolon's commitment to innovation, sustainability, and the beauty of technology.

CHAPTER 21

LEGO House

Billund, Denmark

Bjarke Ingels Group (BIG)

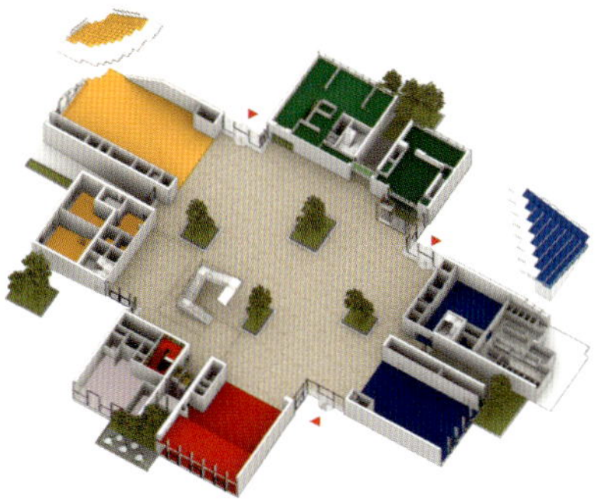

LEGO House in Billund, Denmark, was conceived as a literal manifestation of the infinite LEGO world, an opportunity to demonstrate in a 'real' building how LEGO's famous bricks can be used to create anything the human imagination is capable of rendering, regardless of scale. Is this not a cornerstone of architecture itself? Are not architects children in disguise, only with more sophisticated toys and loftier budgets? If you suspect they are, and if you could select just one building in the world to buttress your case that architects still possess the naivete of children, that their hearts still quicken at the thought of simply *making something*, then you must come here. Because LEGO House is where you can see more clearly than anywhere else that gossamer-thin thread which is all that separates the very young from the, well . . . from the not-so-young.

Bjarke Ingels, the Danish-born architect and founder of the Copenhagen and New York-based BIG, wanted to take the 'clutch' power of the classic 2x4 interlocking hollow-tubed LEGO brick and use its precision and timeless rule of proportions to help people realize new worlds that express more than the everyday. The result? Replicated in a building of what children around the world are doing every day, and in turn have transformed Billund into a new epicentre of fun and learning.

The idea that using LEGO bricks might act as some kind of creative restraint at BIG is dispelled the moment you do the math. Two 2x4 bricks can be combined in 24 different ways, three in 1060 ways, while six 2x4 bricks can be used to make more than 915 million combinations of shapes. For the designers at BIG, lego bricks proved as much a tool as a toy.

Using the Fibonacci Golden Ratio, a numeric system found in nature to efficiently pack cells and plant structures in order to gain the most light and contact with pollinating insects, LEGO House integrates its exhibition and public spaces, embodying the culture and values at the heart of all LEGO experiences. Located in the centre of Billund, the 75 ft high LEGO House is made up of 21 overlapping rectangular volumes that are placed like individual structures set around a 231,424 sq ft LEGO square, precisely lit through the cracks and crevices between each volume. The external walls are not actually bricks but ceramic tiles – over 90,000 of them – clipped onto steel frames in such a way as to mimic the famous 2x4 brick. The internal LEGO Square is cave-like, lacking any columnar support (after all, there are no columns in LEGO) and which is open to the public, permitting visitors to take shortcuts through the building and welcoming passers-by into its café, restaurant, shop and conference spaces. Overhead a cluster of exhibition spaces overlap to create a continuous flow of galleries, each one color-coded to provide a vibrant journey through LEGO's bold rainbow.

There are four play zones on the first and second floors, each defined by its own color and designed to provide activities that reflect a specific aspect of a child's learning: social is green, creative is red, cognitive is blue, emotional is yellow. In the play zones you can create your own stop-motion LEGO movie, build a race car or create a LEGO fish.

One of the most impressive objects is the 'Tree of Creativity'. Constructed using more than 6 million bricks it's one of the largest LEGO structures ever built, taking four months and over 24,000 hours to raise, involving people hanging from the ceiling in harnesses as they glued the upper pieces together. Everywhere you look, Fibonacci's Golden Ratio is evident in the geometry and proportions of the bricks, from the glazed ceramic tiles used in the stairs and internal walls to the pervasive 21 block design, each block, or room being 'suspended' above the plaza thanks to the presence of 1900 tons of steel, engineered to form a sort of bridge from which each block is 'hung'.

The building's upper level is crowned by the uppermost block, the 'keystone', home to the Masterpiece Gallery, a fantastical collection of 'installations' by LEGO fans from around the world made from the 2×4 brick, lit from above from eight circular skylights representing the eight interlocking holes or 'studs' in the LEGO brick. Two corners of the building have a cascading, orthogonal slope that provides both steps and seats with rubberized surfaces for comfort and safety.

Architecturally the subdued white façade of LEGO House is a far cry from the vibrant colors of the nearby LEGO theme park, while the colored floors inside and on the roof are a nod to the standard base plates known to all LEGO users. Pixelated public staircases take you up to rooftop spaces, while on the lower level a History Collection takes visitors on an archival journey through the evolution of the LEGO company. For the LEGO tragic the most exciting space of all, however, is The Vault: a secure area beneath LEGO Square where you can use interactive databases to look up and view the first edition of virtually every LEGO set that's ever been manufactured, including the new 774-piece, 197-step kit that replicates the stacked-block form of LEGO House itself, now available as part of the LEGO Architecture series.

Bjarke Ingels is proud of having created a brick building without once resorting to modifying a brick module, thus keeping to a long-held rule in Dutch construction that says one *never* cuts a masonry brick to fit in with one's design, but rather alter the design to accommodate the brick. He obviously has a rare affinity for this project with its 25 million bricks spread over 130,000 sq feet of immersion and imagination, long a believer in people gaining a sense of empowerment by being able to create their own environment. 'We felt that if BIG had been created to build only one building', he told Frameweb, 'it would be to design the house for LEGO'.

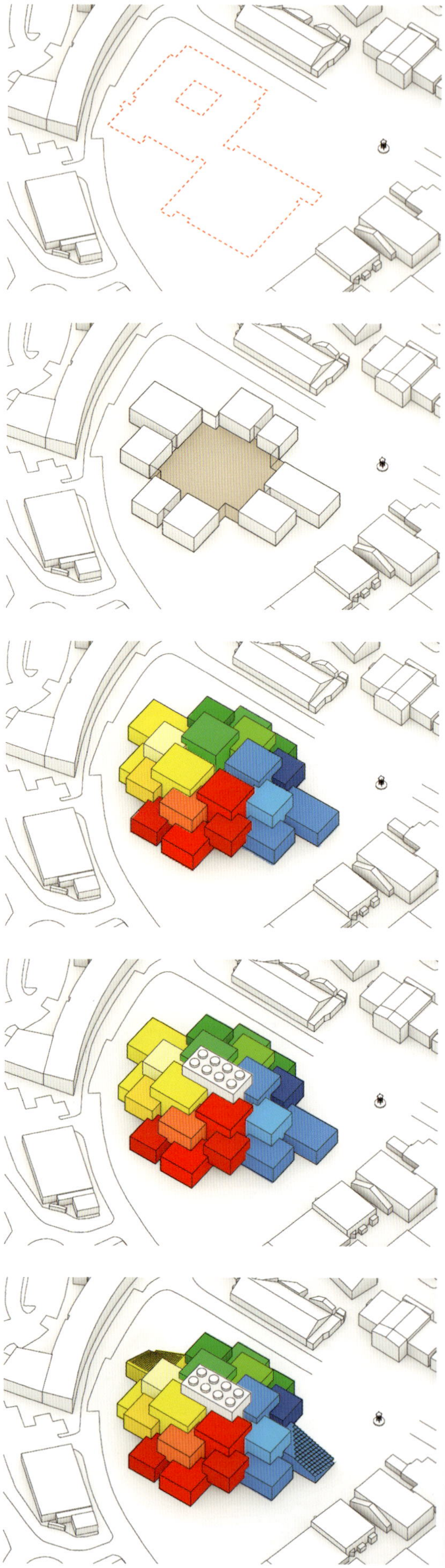

AAHHHH
Lobby
Terrace Red

Green Zone
Grøn Zone
World Explorer

LEGO
History Collection

History Collection
Toilets

CHAPTER 22

Via 57 West

New York City, USA

Bjarke Ingels Group (BIG)

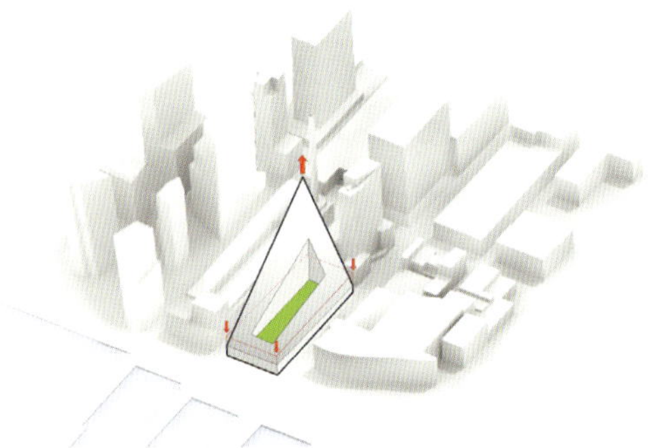

In architecture a perimeter block – a city block or building that rises up on all sides and encloses a private central space or courtyard – is a very 'European' concept. Its design allows for the creation of large urban densities without the need to resort to high-rise structures. Perimeter blocks require two façades: one that faces outwards towards the public space around it, and one facing inwards towards its centre. In Europe, perimeter blocks had their genesis in medieval fortified hill towns, settlements where it was necessary to have strong defensive walls built around 'softer' interiors that were the inhabitant's living spaces – safe and secure open areas that allowed those who lived in a more problematic age to go about their daily lives in relative peace and security.

The fact that VIA 57 West – a luxury residential building in the Manhattan neighborhood of Midtown West – employs such a design concept might be a plus in a city that is the quintessential example of the 'urban jungle', but is only one of the reasons why this building is gaining so much attention. A striking hybrid between the perimeter blocks of Europe and the Manhattan high-rise, it has the advantages of both: all of the compactness demanded by its necessarily restricted footprint, the benefits of a courtyard building, and the openness and expansive views of a typical skyscraper.

The inaugural architectural project in North America by the Danish architectural firm BIG, VIA 57 West's unique pyramid shape has at its centre a striking 22,000 square foot sloping courtyard garden, providing residents with views out to the Hudson River. Its north-east corner dramatically rises up to its 450 ft peak, with its remaining three corners low to the ground, thus opening its interior to the west and allowing the late afternoon sun to flood its core with light. And the garden was no mere afterthought, possessing the same emphasis as seen in Frederick Law Olmsted's Central Park, a few blocks to the east. While it might be thousands of times smaller, the concept is the same, with its sunny and open grass-like meadow to the west contrasting with its more leafy east, an emerging forest in miniature filled with almost a hundred trees and 50 species of native plants.

The garden follows a notable trend throughout the city in recent years that has seen an emphasis on providing more green spaces, whether it be the High Line in the Meatpacking District or the new park lands further south along the Hudson River. The garden may be a private retreat for the building's residents, connected to the foyer with its walls of angular brick via a grand staircase, but as its trees mature they will become increasingly more visible from the city, providing a connection to the green spaces of the 550-acre Hudson River Park, the nation's longest riverfront park.

If you're fortunate enough to be a resident of VIA 57 West you'll want for nothing. There's a half basketball court, gymnasium, game rooms with table tennis tables, pool tables, multiple sun decks, and even rooms for poker as well as a golf simulator, cinema and swimming pool, all of which are concentrated around the courtyard and so providing a stimulating social hub. Above, apartments are awash in oak wood floors and cabinetry, solar shades, and are always oriented towards the wide, placid waters of the Hudson River.

Complimenting the building's main entry is 'Flows Two Ways', a sinuous blurring of façade and sculpture by the Los Angeles-based Stephen Glassman Studio. Hailed by *Architect's Newspaper* as 'the most innovative New York City wall work in nearly fifty years', this mesmerising eight-story high installation of stainless steel, aluminium and rolled metal evokes the gentle movements of the nearby river and has the power to fairly stop you in your tracks when you pass it by. 'Flows Two Ways' is a loose translation of the river's Native American name of *muh-he-kun-ne-tuk* – the 'river that flows both ways' – and illustrates Glassman's love of art that is socially constructive but also has a little of what he likes to call 'aesthetic anarchy'.

In 2016 the Council on Tall Buildings and Urban Habitat (CTBUH) named VIA 57 West the Best Tall Building in the Americas. But a tall building that is what? A warped pyramid? A hyperbolic paraboloid? Maybe a tetrahedral? Set in a skyline known the world over for its square and rectangular shapes, this is a dramatic departure from the skyscraper image which began in Chicago and reached its zenith above the Manhattan schist bedrock that makes the weighty cityscape of Midtown possible. Its 32 storys represent nothing less than a new typology for the city, and is a building that never stops altering its appearance, its form shifting depending upon your vantage point. From the West Side Highway it resembles a pyramid, but when on West 58th Street it transforms into a glass spire, a gleaming, pointy example of New York Modern.

There are 178 distinct floor plans in the 709 apartments at VIA 57 West, a diversity made possible, if not downright unavoidable, by its angled design composed of a simple ruled surface. Every apartment has its own bay window, amplifying the generous views.

VIA 57 West doesn't just look good, it has a conscience too. The building recycles more than 60,000 gallons of water every day, while the wood in its internal surfaces has been carefully sourced from responsibly grown forests. Its angled shape also makes it a good neighbor, graciously allowing for the views over the Hudson River long held by residents in the adjacent 38-story Helena Towers, itself a pioneering building in the pursuit of environmental excellence, to be retained.

In fact there's not a box left unticked in its pursuit to satisfy, well, *everyone* – designers, town planners, nervous neighbors, environmentalists, its own residents – and doing it all with aplomb in the toughest real estate market in the world.

And that's no mean feat.

BIG IDEAS:
SMALL BUILDINGS

CHAPTER 23

Tiny Tower

Philadelphia, USA

Interface Studio Architects (ISA)

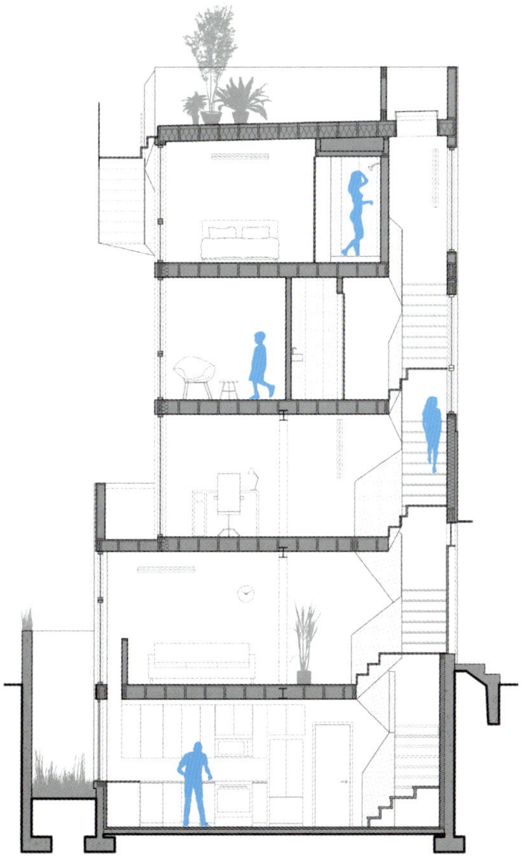

The US city of Philadelphia has trodden a rocky path over the decades. It's had a declining population for some 50 years. It's the poorest large city in the country, and has endured persistent and, at times, debilitating periods of stagnant economic growth. But now there is new hope in America's sixth-largest city, founded by William Penn in 1682 and home to the Liberty Bell and Independence Hall. The city's population is growing again, albeit slowly, and a building boom is underway that is bringing new life to the city skyline. But what's exciting isn't limited to what's happening to its CBD and rising skyscrapers. CBD skylines always look after themselves. It's what's happening in neighborhoods that are still struggling to throw off the shackles of economic downturns. It's what's happening in places like the old Brewerytown district, once filled with more than its share of derelict buildings but now experiencing an exciting new era of regeneration, that's getting people talking.

There isn't a city in the world that doesn't have a glut of leftover building sites so small as to be considered virtually unbuildable. But the days when small was thought unusable are gone. Small lots of fallow land, common sights in every urban centre, are now being looked at afresh, thanks in part to architects like Brian Phillips, Principal at the Philadelphia-based firm Interface Studio Architects (ISA).

The plot on which ISA's Tiny Tower now sits redefines real estate 'small'. At just 29 feet long and under 12 feet wide this prototype building promises to unlock the development potential of small sites everywhere. It will inspire town planners to cast a fresh eye toward hitherto overlooked sites that might be considered for the construction of low-cost housing, particularly in cities like Philadelphia where its supply has long been at a premium.

At 38 feet high, Tiny Tower maximizes its footprint. It is an elegant, slender five story home with the kitchen and bathroom on the ground floor, which sits slightly below grade. The living room is above as well as an office which comes with a small balcony. Above them are two bedrooms, each with their own bathroom.

Tiny Tower might be small, but it reflects in miniature the principles of skyscraper design with its different levels connected by a core of vertical circulation courtesy of its folded steel plate staircase. Its steel-reinforced timber frame is wrapped in metal sheeting, and a two-story embedded steel frame helps to stabilize the building's extended verticality.

The staircase deserves special mention. The single most important design element in a building where space is such a luxury, it is here that the designers at ISA have excelled with a folded-plate, light-filled steel staircase that connects all five levels. The siting of it on the building's perimeter frees up the rest of the building to become well-lit living spaces, while a separate external stairway provides access to the roof.

It is hoped that future changes to design and zoning policies in Philadelphia will free up more sites for the construction of similar flexible-use buildings and increasingly affordable housing. Brian Phillips likes to call new homes that can be built for less than US$100,000 'urban cabins'. 'In Philadelphia, whether you're rich or poor', he said while being interviewed at the Harvard Joint Center for Housing Studies in 2018, 'you're probably living in a 16ft-wide house'.

In 2015 ISA was named an 'Emerging Voice' in architecture by the Architectural League of New York, an acknowledgement that not only does ISA now have a large body of realized and celebrated work, but also what they are doing has significance beyond simply that of design. Tiny Tower reminds us that architecture must have at its heart a social conscience, an ability to alter our environment for the greater good of all.

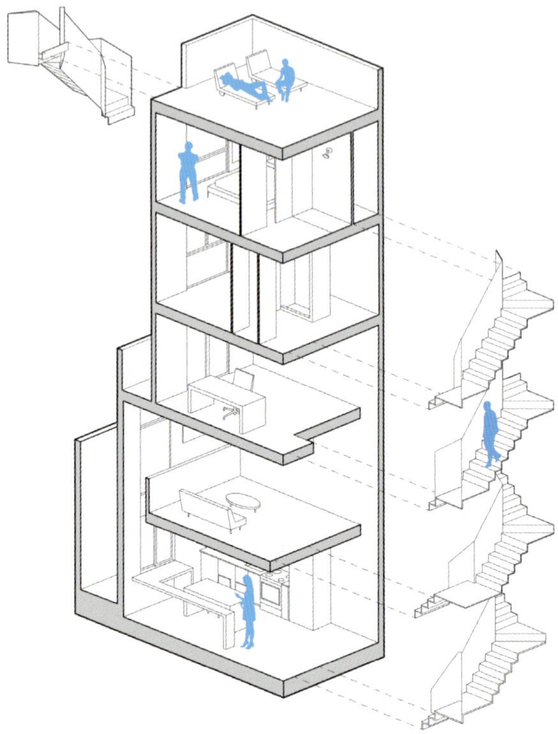

CHAPTER 24

Freebooter

Amsterdam, Holland

GG-loop

Biophilic architecture. If you're not familiar with the term then you're certainly not alone. But it wouldn't hurt to get acquainted. Because if Freebooter, a pair of prefabricated apartments designed by the Amsterdam-based architecture studio GG-loop are any guide, there's going to be a whole lot more of it in years to come. First popularized by the American theorist, biologist and two time Pulitzer Prize-winner for General Nonfiction Edward Wilson in his 1984 book of the same name, biophilia argues that humans have a natural inclination to immerse themselves in nature, that we possess an inescapable affection for the world around us that lays rooted in our evolutionary biology. So what do two 1313 square feet apartments on the north-east of Zeeburgereiland, a triangular island in Amsterdam's IJ River, have to do with biophilic theory and humanity's innate connection to the natural world?

Freebooter – a word given to describe an old time pirate, plunderer, and no doubt a reference to the many anti-heroes found throughout Holland's proud maritime past – combines environmental features with natural shapes and forms, imitating the concepts that are commonly found in nature's living systems. It's floorplan was designed to 'unfold' before you, its organic lines creating wonderfully fluid spaces. Everything you see, all of its cross-laminated timbers (CLT) and western red cedar and the steel in its frame, were pre-fabricated. The overall construction period spanned six months, and it took just three weeks to assemble the structures four floors onsite. And while its external vertical slats create a double façade and are there to provide its occupants with shade and privacy, they are not *too* close together. A perfect blend of transparency and seclusion, they are a reminder that this is a country with an odd dislike for traditional curtains, an outward manifestation of the Dutch idea that its people have nothing to hide.

GG-loop's founder, Italian-born Giacomo Garziano, spent a year looking at how sunlight fell on this corner block and how best to position its slats to allow in light and to create its striking parametric shape. Once inside and you're able to see how natural light illuminates its open spaces and private niches, it becomes obvious it was a year well spent.

Apartment #1 includes a 538 square foot garden, 269 square feet of outdoor space, 86 square feet of balcony and a single car space. Apartment #2, the upper apartment, has a 323 square foot roof terrace, 226 square feet of additional terraces, 215 square feet of balcony and a single car space. Both apartments possess a central core that contains the kitchen, bathroom and toilets, surrounding them are the 'resting areas' including a master bedroom, single bedroom and study, and the living and dining areas beyond them. The stairways are ladder-like, while cut-outs in the pine-clad internal walls echo the interiors of ship cabins. Everywhere here there are hints to the country's maritime past, from the use of wood to create a sense of standing on a ship's deck to the alternating height of each room according to its function, an age-old principle of ship design.

In a city where real estate in the CBD has risen markedly in recent years it makes sense to build in places like Zeeburgereiland, which in the past two decades has been transformed from an industrial precinct to a sought-after residential community where architects feel less restrained to imitate the red brick typology that has long been Amsterdam's signature look. The island certainly mimics the changing times. A hundred years ago it wasn't even here, laying underwater, its location a thoroughfare for the ships of the Dutch navy. A creation of the river's accumulating sediments, Zeeburgereiland has risen out of nothing to become a talking point in one of Europe's most vibrant cities.

As have the architects at GG-loop.

CHAPTER 25

The 7th Room

Harads, Sweden

Snøhetta

Four hours by train north of Stockholm, tucked away in a forest of pines just below the Arctic Circle near the town of Harads, is a pioneering concept in hotel accommodation: Treehotel. Opened in 2010 there are seven tree houses here: each of them unique, each designed by different architects so to avoid even a hint of repetition. They are: The Bird's Nest, The Cabin, The Mirrorcube, The UFO, The Dragonfly, The Blue Cone, and the most recent and visually stunning of them all – The 7th Room.

The Bird Cage has an exterior of twigs and branches and was inspired by sea eagle's nests that Treehotel's owner had seen while salmon fishing in eastern Siberia. Mirrorcube measures 13 x 13 x 13 feet and is clad in reflective glass. The Cabin's roof doubles as an outdoor terrace. The UFO is accessed by a metal ladder that descends from the suspended, saucer-shaped object much like one would in a 1950s science-fiction movie. You won't find any nails in the trunks or branches of any of the pods at Treehotel. Everything is held aloft by a combination of slender steel posts and multiple

trunk-hugging adjustable brackets that can be made larger as the trees grow. All are accessed via a mix of staircases, ramps, descending manual and mechanized ladders, or rope bridges. All of their toilets burn waste into ashes, their floors are heated, and lighting is courtesy of low energy LED's. Interiors are filled with Scandinavian-inspired furniture and storage spaces, and once you're inside any of them, the sense of solitude is tangible.

And not for a single moment do you forget just where you are.

Because when the wind blows, the trees move … *you* move.

It all began when Kent and partner Britta came to the small town of Harads and purchased the derelict shell of a 1940s retirement home, a *Pensionat,* giving it new life as a guesthouse and which now doubles as Treehotel's reception and restaurant. Meals are taken in the *Pensionat* and are cooked by Britta and Sebastian, a local chef who dislikes big restaurants and is at home with Treehotel's philosophy of unpretentious hospitality. On the menu you'll find moose stew with baked potatoes, and Arctic Char, which is like Atlantic salmon. Only better. A quarter mile path takes you from the *Pensionat* to the edge of their treehouse-filled forest.

The 7th Room is the largest of the structures here and the most recent installation. It is also the only room that is freestanding. Designed by Oslo-based international design firm Snøhetta, it sits 33 feet above the ground, held aloft by twelve slender steel columns. An industrial-looking steel staircase provides access and there's a small and very welcome electric lift for your baggage. The first thing you'll notice, however, when you look up from beneath is a life-size photograph depicting the canopy here as it was prior to the room being constructed – a disorienting act of camouflage artfully printed onto a single vast sheet of aluminium that spans the entire underside of the cabin. Snøhetta like to call it the room's 'sixth façade'.

On the outside the pine cladding, which harkens back to traditional expressions of Nordic gabled design, has been charred black in order to create a maintenance-free exterior. On the inside birch plywood has been used on its internal walls, and its flooring is ash – a light timbered, almost typically 'blonde' Swedish feel, contrasting with its dark exterior. 800 square feet of internal living space includes two bedrooms, a sunken living area, modern kitchen and bathroom with a delightful hallway linking it all. Floor to ceiling windows make full use of the Arctic's long summer days with views extending over forests and the nearby Lule River.

Everywhere you look its living spaces possess all of the crisp, clean lines of minimalist chic. The bedrooms, their beds embedded into the floor, have rectangular skylights for when the sun goes down. Snøhetta collaborated with avant-garde lighting designers Ateljé Lyktan to produce some beautiful birch veneer lamps – a suspended light in the sunken lounge, and a mounted light in each bedroom. There's a wood burning stove just off from the sunken lounge, and don't think for one moment that those Scandia-looking swivel chairs in the hallway are mere copies of the Hans Brattrud-designed laminated masterpiece. They're the real thing.

Outside, a dramatic installation of heavy rope netting creates a suspended balcony that can be accessed from both bedrooms and the hallway, making it an omnipresent, floating extension, always inviting, always beckoning you to walk out onto its bobbing, textured, knotted surface. Attached to the 7th Room and also to a single, towering pine

tree that rises up through its centre, the balcony is the most sure-fire antidote to vertigo you'll ever see. It's simply impossible not to want to be on it, and is the perfect place to unfurl a sleeping bag for the ultimate night under the stars. When the Northern Lights make their inevitable appearance, it provides one more vantage point in a cabin with no shortage of windows onto the heavens above.

The latest addition to Treehotel, the 'Arctic Bath' (with architecture and design by Bertil Harström and Johan Kauppi) will open by the end of 2019. Sweden's first floating spa and sister property to Treehotel on the nearby Lule River, Arctic Bath will be a monument to the Swedish 'timber floating' era when forests were culled and their trees floated down its rivers to be milled. Designed to float in summer and freeze into place in winter, its circular shape will surround a central bath/spa/plunge pool, the 4 degree Lule River itself. Heated to 39 degrees Fahrenheit to prevent it from freezing, the spa will be encircled by saunas and relaxation rooms, with an exterior clad in a riotous display of locally milled logs, rising up in a random looking crunch reminiscent of a 'log-jam' that was once a common sight on this old logging river. Arctic Bath is the perfect watery accompaniment to The 7th Room; the latest manifestation of Treehotel's on-going experiment on how inspiring architecture can soften humankind's encroachment on the realm of nature.

SONHA

CHAPTER 26

BRICK CAVE

Thụy Lâm, Vietnam

H&P Architects

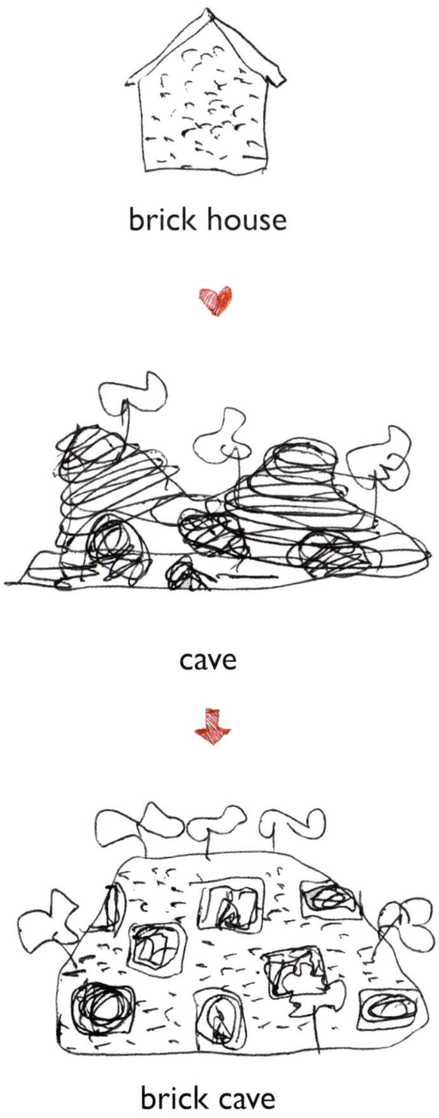

Thụy Lâm is a typical suburban commune to the north of the Vietnamese capital of Hanoi, a former farming area which, like many rural areas across the country is slowly succumbing to the nation's increasing urban sprawl. In response, architects are grappling with how to incorporate landscapes into its buildings in a society that is in danger of losing touch with the natural environment. One approach, taken by Hanoi-based H&P Architects, was to build a perforated brick wall right on the outer edge of a small urban block in Thụy Lâm, making use of the entire site's 1884 square foot footprint, then raise a second internal wall, the two separated by what could best be described as your own personal alleyway. The outer wall is perpendicular to a height of 8.37 feet, then inclines inwards to a height of 25.5 feet. The roof is flat and home to a rooftop garden. The external façade's metamorphosis from perpendicular to angular gives the building the appearance of wrapping back in on itself, while its perforated walls and generous windows maintain a connection to the streets beyond, its double-walled exterior filtering sun, noise, light and moisture, a beguiling mix of darkness and light. An urban cave.

Rarely has the simplicity of the humble brick, long preferred as a building material in Vietnam because of its profligacy and low cost, been used to create such an aesthetic urban oasis, the sheer variety of its patterns providing not even a hint of uniformity. The outer wall's incline produces some interesting triangular-shaped internal walls, while effectively reducing the building's considerable volume.

Internal walls, both structural and dividing, are connected to its external walls via a system of rooftop girders. The entire ground floor is an expansive living area, bedrooms and sitting rooms are on the first floor, and on the roof is the garden complete with its own water cistern. The walkway between the two external walls allows for more greenery in a garden area that can be as high as the building itself, capable of growing not just shrubs but trees, their branches trained to protrude through Brick Cave's angled façades. The house has modern air conditioning of course, but with this much brick to act as a natural insulator as well as plants arranged in its plentiful nooks and crevices to soak up humidity, it is rarely used.

The assymetrical internal design allows for some truly delightful spaces, such as first floor balconies that look down onto the ground floor and above into soaring, atrium-like spaces lit by hundreds of random apertures, the tiny spaces left open in between each of its locally sourced bricks. And this is perhaps Brick Cave's most endearing legacy, that traditional materials such as bricks can always be reinvented, that common, vernacular architecture and the materials that compose it are never more than a few degrees of separation away from meaningful architecture.

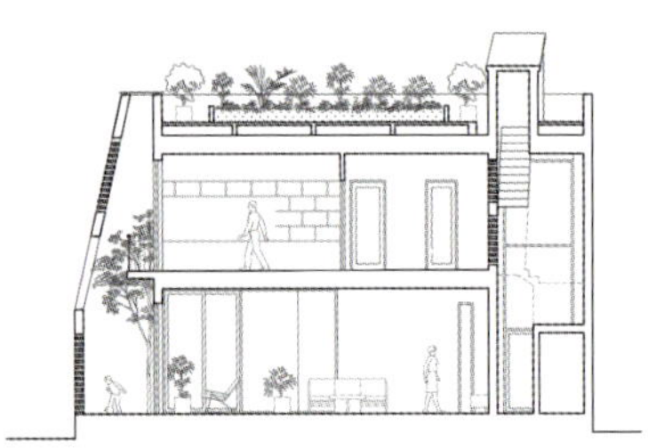

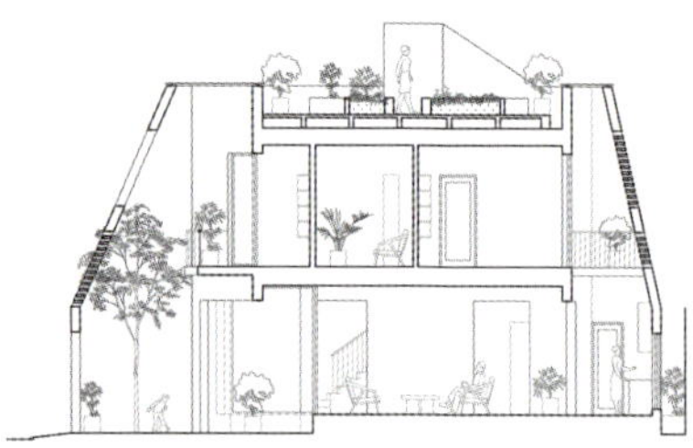

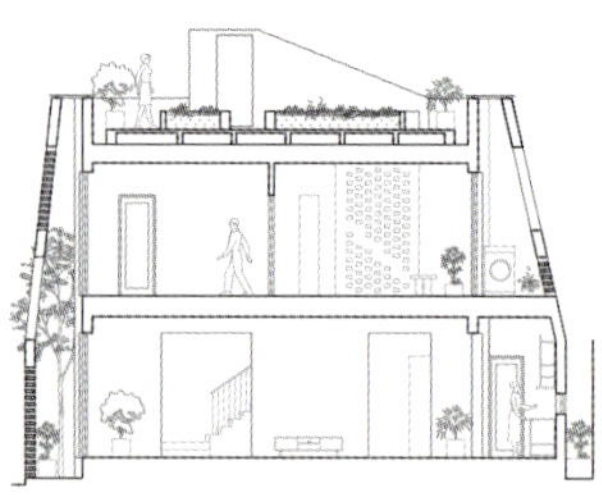

CHAPTER 27

Don Juan House

Don Juan, Ecuador

Emilio López Arquitecto

Don Juan House, located in the town of the same name to the west of the Ecuadorian capital Quito on the Pacific coast, is a breath of fresh architectural air, a private home in the form of a bow-tie when viewed from above. Its two funnel-like boxes merge together to create a beautiful geometric form, with an interior spread over two levels. With each of its glazed façades entirely open to the views beyond they look like giant lightboxes, two vast lenses always open, always in a perpetual state of readiness. Apertures poised to provide its occupants with the perfect snapshot over whatever it is that nature can conjure.

On the ground floor there is the kitchen, dining room, living room and a bathroom. At the rear another wall of double-height windows contains a staircase with a simple platform at its mid-way point that takes you up to the two ocean-facing bedrooms and extra bathroom. These float above almost unnoticed in their loft-like isolation, peering down over the living spaces below.

The floorplan is simple, straightforward, functional – as are the materials used in its construction. You'll find no hi-tech elements here. Don Juan House is testimony to how age-old materials never go out of fashion. In an era where there is much debate surrounding the affordability of architecture, with its over-engineered CAD-designed spaces and seemingly never-ending array of new composites adding complexity and new possibilities – and of course, added cost. But in Don Juan House all you have is simplicity: uncluttered, affordable simplicity. Which surely must result in a contented and uncluttered mind?

Don Juan House is constructed from locally sourced timbers, mostly Amarillo or 'Canary Wood', a heavy wood which is also surprisingly easy to work with, and resistant to insects and fungi. The exterior is clad in flat fibre-cement panels, with the panel's interior faces plastered over and then covered in the warmth and strength of bamboo.

Sitting atop its own little hill above the coastal town of Don Juan, the house is oriented east-west to take advantage of sunrises and sunsets, the ocean on one side and a deciduous forest on the other. Its design allows for cross-ventilation thanks to

a profusion of sliding glass doors, and an ocean-facing outdoor deck makes the views over the coastline below seem even more visceral. All of the cabinetry in the house is unashamedly wood based, which adds to its sense of unity and purpose – making a statement that wood alone as a construction and aesthetic material is enough. It needs no ornamentation, no embellishment.

The verticality of the external side windows accentuate the soaring spaces within, while the exposed horizontal framework on the internal walls provides a sense of depth, strength and – if you care to look at it this way – an ode to buildings everywhere that were built by carpenters and everyday people using materials common to their environment. This is a *vernacular* building. Vernacular architecture – buildings that are designed to suit local environments – are made by ordinary and often unskilled people using local products and so are not by definition designed or built by architects. But look more closely at what Emilio López has wrought here. He has achieved a fusion of the vernacular and the architectural. He has given hope to builders and carpenters and hobbyists everywhere that a beautiful, functional building can be made mixing traditional elements with imaginative flair, and that it can still be capable of stopping a passerby in their tracks, to take a second look.

CHAPTER 28

Patio House

Karpathos, Greece

OOAK Architects

Closer to mainland Turkey than it is to Greece, the island of Karpathos lies in the southeastern Aegean Sea on the boundary of the Sea of Crete, a sub-basin of the Mediterranean. It is an isolated island whose communities cling fiercly to old customs and dialects, its festivals a celebration of local dance, music and food, while all around them a ring of twenty beaches such as sandy Kyra Panagia and pebbly Achata enchant you with warm waters that alternate from emerald green to azure blue. Karpathos has yet to give itself up to mass tourism. Solitude is still easy to find. So if you're looking to build your dream house on one of the 227 inhabited Greek islands that are scattered throughout the Aegean and Ionian seas, don't make a decision until you've come here.

That's what the French/Swedish couple who built Patio House did. They came here and found their dream location on a windy Karpathos cliff overlooking Afiarti beach, a dramatic site with the Aegean Sea open before them.

The raw, uncompromising landscape dictated the design that was to come. Every man-made change to the landscape would be seen here, so decisions had to be taken in how to best introduce a massed concrete volume into a world of jagged, precipitous cliffs. In the end it was decided it was pointless to try and mimic the landscape, with the house instead placed as gently as one could onto the site with minimal impact upon the surrounding landscape. Here, topography and building are seen as two separate elements which when seen together create a new reality, each one enhancing the other, two contrasting objects existing in symbiosis together.

The site comprises two natural plateaus, one above the other, with the building extending out over the higher plateau, floating above the landscape, to reach out towards the sea and take full advantage of endless Aegean views. This bold cantilever projects an overwhelming presence, while creating the illusion from inside its living spaces that the house is hovering above the water.

The owners wanted Patio House to be a true sanctuary, a place where they could immerse themselves in the landscape while at the same time shelter from the island's strong winds. The building's core is a single story arranged around an inner patio, with

a series of voids blurring the distinction between what is inside and what lies beyond. Another void through the building connects it to an outdoor terrace on the plateau below, while a section up from the single-story is raised to allow for height differences, while at the same time creating an independent space for visitors. There are stone tiles on its floors, an open-air dining area, and every room including its two bedrooms, master suite and living areas feature seriously large windows designed to frame distant horizons.

In Patio House, OOAK have achieved what they set out to accomplish, a massed volume of cast in-situ reinforced concrete with a textured, board-marked finish that is at once a retreat, a home, and with such minimal impact upon its site that it adds to, rather than subtracts from, the rock-strewn landscape it inhabits.

CHAPTER 29

Klein A45

Shandaken, USA

Søren Rose & Bjarke Ingels Group (BIG)

It should come as no surprise that when the Danish designer Søren Rose teamed up with the internationally renowned architectural firm Bjarke Ingels Group (BIG) to create something very small, that they'd still manage to pull off a very 'big' statement. If you're the sort who longs for the simple life, whose pulse doesn't quicken at the thought of painting windows, repairing façades or mowing lawns, who yearns for a lifestyle where you've the time to pursue the things you like, then this could well be the tiny house of your dreams. It's ingenious design is a bold new take on the traditional A-frame home, the limitations of which, as everyone who has ever owned one knows only too well, is that there's very little space around the edges. Angled walls encroach into living spaces and are just, well . . . annoying. Rose and BIG began with a square, then took two of the roof's corners and stretched them way, way up, while at the same time taking the other two and have them plummet floorwards, 'twisting' the internal space through 45 degrees into a prism-like form which gives it an ever-changing appearance when viewed from outside.

What it lacks in floor area (180 sq feet) it ably makes up for in ceiling height, which tops out at an impressive 13 ft, thus providing a surprising sense of space that can even include a small loft. So to all those out there who might have always wanted that perfect weekend getaway, or whose budgets simply might not allow for a more traditional home, bid farewell to stultifying angled walls and predictably pitched rooflines. And say hello to the A45.

The first in a series of prototypes to be built in Upstate New York, A45 has an exposed solid pine timber frame, cork walls for insulation, and a Douglas Fir floor. It can be ordered, customized and constructed in around 4 to 6 months in any location and for a variety of purposes, and assembled on site from flat-packed modules utilizing 100 percent recycled materials. Its interior is bathed in natural daylight courtesy of its striking triangular floor-to-ceiling window, made up of seven separate pieces of glass.

People talk of the A45 as being 'acoustic', of having a heart courtesy of its Morsøe wood-burning fireplace. Its interior space certainly reflects the Danish concept of *hygge*, a word with no precise English translation but which means a sense of contentment and well-being, an ideal feeling or a moment one can experience whether alone or with friends. That's what A45 fosters – the art of creating intimacy.

Off-the-grid equipment includes batteries and solar power cells that are tucked away at the back. Inside, a petite Københavns Møbelsnedkeri kitchen compliments hand-crafted Carl Hansen furniture. The bed is fitted with Kvadrat fabric and there's cedar wood in the bathroom. Beneath the subfloor, four concrete piers elevate the structure above the ground, thus allowing its owners to site it in in remote areas without having to bring in excavators or heavy machinery. It's exterior timbers, sourced from the sustainable timber supply firm Dinesen, are available in natural cedar or burnt pine, a firing technique which provides the timber's external face with a carbon crust that is UV and weather resistant.

A long-term goal of Søren Rose is to develop a series of sustainable tiny houses in cooperation with some of the world's leading architects. With A45, he is off to a triumphant start.

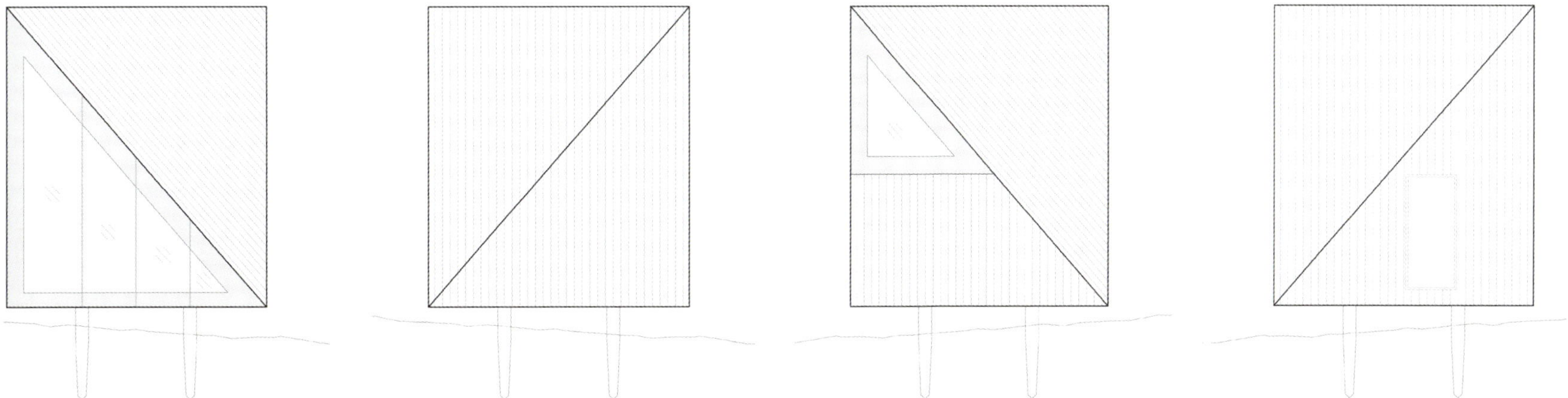

CHAPTER 30

The Skywalk

Gibraltar

Mayice Studio and Arc Designs

It was once a British World War II-era anti-aircraft platform, located high in what is now the Upper Rock Nature Reserve on Gibraltar. Its gun, installed in 1901, could fire a shell capable of hitting the North African coast. But this relic of another age has now given up its lofty vantage point to a far more agreeable structure. The Skywalk is the latest attraction built here on behalf of the Government of Gibraltar in a series of improvements aimed at providing visitors with new perspectives from atop one of the world's most recognisable summits. Part of a wider master plan, The Skywalk compliments a new 230 foot long bridge – the Windsor Suspension Bridge – as well as the restoration of various former military batteries, installations, and newly established walking trails.

Located on one of the highest points of the Rock and one of the few spots that affords views both to the east and west, there's no better place to look over a landscape where two different worlds (Europe and Africa) converge, and is a welcome break as you climb Douglas Path on your way up to O'Hara's Battery, the Rock's highest point.

The designer's over-riding vision was to provide the visitor with a panorama of unrivalled views in every direction – including down over the rocky cliff-face beneath – while being mindful of the project's impact on what is a fragile environment ... to create a subtle intervention which would not detract from the site's unique setting. The use of cantilevered walkways with glazed flooring and balustrading limits the intrusion of solid materials that would otherwise obstruct lines of sight; steel stairways give access to the original military platform and octagonal concrete gun-base which has been redeveloped with seating to allow weary visitors to rest and contemplate distant horizons.

The state-of-the-art Skywalk has a 8 foot wide walkway which hovers above the precipitous terrain, its fully glazed floor unnervingly maximising views and causing hearts to flutter. The structure is secured to the rock with anchors, each of which can support a tensile load of 15 tons, allowing it to not only withstand truckloads of visitors but also the Rock's considerable wind speeds, which can be as much as 95 mph. For those who may be unable or simply not in the mood to take the stairs, a fully glazed

panoramic lift provides an alternative means of access and is an integral part of the design.

With vehicular access to the site limited by necessarily narrow and winding roads, the entire structure was prefabricated in a series of small sections then transported and assembled together on site, a challenging prospect when you're working in a tight, at times near-vertical space at the mercy of weather conditions that can change for the worse in minutes. Construction was further limited by having to use smallish cranes due to the age of the original military platform on which they needed to be placed. The primary steel structure is made up of 18 separate pieces with a combined weight of over 33 tons and would have been even heavier if the vertical steel panels on its stairways weren't perforated, a must-have design element that lessens the structure's visual impact and allows the calming, azure hues of the Atlantic Ocean on one side and the Mediterranean Sea on the other to delightfully infiltrate its every delightful aspect.

And calming might indeed be required. The Skywalk juts out some 1115 feet above sea-level, higher than the Eiffel Tower and three times the height of New York's Statue of Liberty, the glazed components alone accruing to more than 8070 square feet of glass panels, the equivalent of four tennis courts, the largest weighing some 1400 pounds. It's almost as though it isn't there at all, a fact that will test the tendency to vertigo of all who come here.

Mark Hamill, the actor who played the now mythic character Luke Skywalker in the *Star Wars* movie franchise was on hand to open it, dressed in black trousers and a camel overcoat and using his vaunted light sabre to symbolically slash at the red ribbon that was stretched across the Skywalk's transparent platform as two Stormtroopers looked on. Appropriate enough symbolism, perhaps, for a Rebel lookout lookout which, once you're on it, can lift you up out of yourself, maybe even make you feel a little Jedi-like, and briefly at least help us see beyond the confines of our earthly lives.

CHAPTER 31

Tunnel of Light

Niigata, Japan

MAD Architects

Throughout the 20th century Japan's population did what most of the world's did. It grew. From 45 million in 1900 to 128 million in 2000. Since then, however, birth rates have plummeted. More than half its population is now 46 years or older, a statistic that makes it the world's oldest large country. It's estimated the population, now at 127 million, will fall to just 106 million by 2040, and nowhere is this shift in numbers more visible than in its rural areas as young people drift towards its sprawling urban areas in search of work. In response, government authorities are initialising projects which, it is hoped, will help address its demographic challenges. One such project is the restoration of the 2460 foot-long Kiyotsu Gorge Tunnel in the heart of the Niigata Prefecture on the west coast of Honshu Island.

The tunnel, given a stunning makeover by MAD Architects in 2018 is now a permanent art installation, created for the Echigo-Tsumari Art Triennale, an outdoor program designed to facilitate the integration of people into nature, with as many as 200 artworks spread over the 293 square miles of the Echigo-Tsumari Art Field.

MAD's design draws upon the five elements of nature – wood, earth, metal, fire and water. It begins with the first installation, a small wooden hut near to the tunnel's entrance, home to a cafe and souvenir shop on its ground floor while above a soaring cedar-clad roof with a central aperture (nicknamed the 'periscope') allows light to fall onto a circular hot spring foot spa below. The aperture is topped by a series of mirrored lenses, angled to reflect the surrounding gorge. This is 'Wood'.

Entering the tunnel proper you are pulled out of reality and into a world that is bathed in color, depth, and unexpectedly lit spaces. Progressing along its restored entrance, illuminated with a series of mesmerizing colored lights augmented with an appropriate selection of ephemeral music, you begin your journey into a realm with an ambiance that is infused with a rare dynamism. This is 'Earth'. Next is the Invisible Bubble, the first of the tunnel's four lookout points. One cannot doubt its functionality (it is a toilet), but even here there's an element of the other-worldly with its transparent wall that faces the gorge covered in a one-way metallic film, ensuring privacy. This is

'Metal'. Then comes The Drop, a series of molten-like, illuminated 'droplets' suspended in the wall and ceiling, reflective openings backlit by orangey/red lighting. This is 'Fire'.

Finally there is the tunnel's grand finale, its end, its inevitable culmination. It draws you forward in a sort of hypnotic state, unable to resist its lure. The tunnel's walls are now lined by sheets of reflective, semi-polished stainless steel that seem to suck in the V-shaped gorge's rock formations beyond and all the greenery that clings to them. A reflecting pool is also now at your feet, further reflecting the images about you in a kaleidoscope of upside-down panoramas. This is 'Water'.

No more a dewy, dank and dark abandoned place, the Kiyotsu Gorge Tunnel is now a place of reflection, even of pilgrimage, that will immerse you in Echigo-Tsumari's spirit of infinite nature.

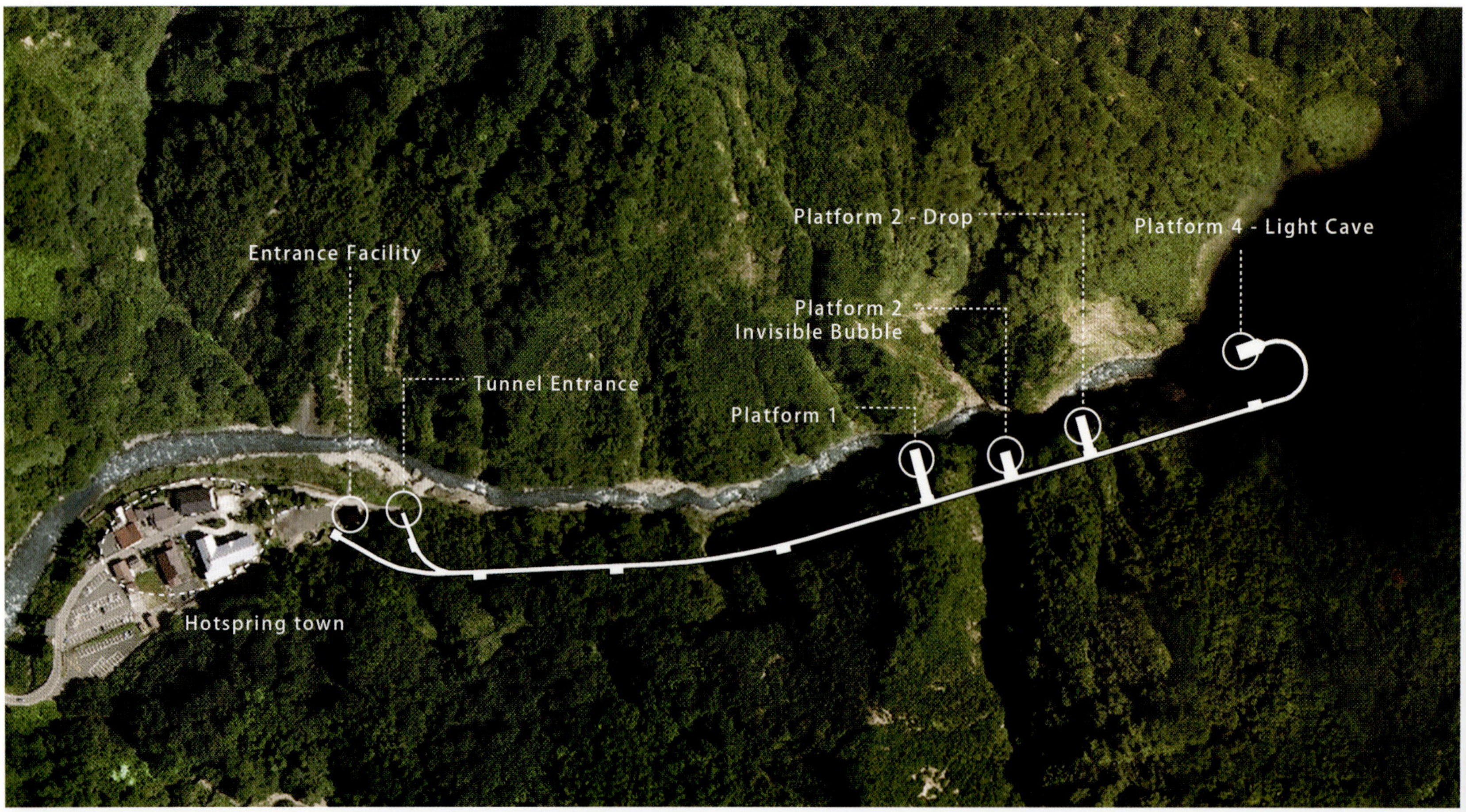

CHAPTER 32

Norwegian Wild Reindeer Pavilion

Hjerkinn, Norway

Snøhetta

The Dovrefjell mountain range in Norway is the country's great natural barrier, an alpine region separating its greener, more verdant south from the frigid tundra landscapes to its north. Dovrefjell-Sunndalsfjella National Park was established in 2002 and protects in excess of 1660 square miles of this pristine environment, home to the arctic fox, and to musk oxen which died out in Norway during the last Ice Age but now thrive here once more after their reintroduction from Greenland in the 1930s and 40s. The park is also home to Europe's last remaining herd of wild mountain reindeer. What better place in all of continental Europe could there be to build a viewing platform from which one can look out in comfort, and see nature as it used to be?

Designed by the Oslo-based architectural firm Snøhetta, who took their name from the highest mountain in the Dovrefjell range at 7500 feet, the 970 square foot Wild Reindeer Pavilion is in many ways a straightforward construction and very Norwegian in its concept – uncomplicated, functional, welcoming. Situated on a 3937 foot-high plateau in Hjerkinn on the cusp of Dovrefjell-Sunndalsfjella National Park looking towards the triple peaks of Snøhetta, it is accessed via a 1 mile-long hiking trail and is open year round to the public. A suspended furnace provides warmth to a curvaceous, organically timbered interior that is tucked snugly behind a panoramic expanse of floor to ceiling glass supported on a series of slender steel fins.

The internal 10 inch square beams were individually milled by shipbuilders in nearby Hardangerfjord on a CNC machine using digital 3D modeling, and assembled using wooden pegs to create its striking wave-like appearance. Its interior resembles a topographical map, a time-worn representation of the valley and mountains over which it looks, a 'liquid wood' sculpted and smoothed by eons of erosion by wind and rain. Spread over three tiers, it is an architectural composition of the highest order.

The pavilion's exterior, by contrast, is a robust rectangular frame of unprocessed, rusted steel, the color of which blends harmoniously with the iron found in the rock of

the surrounding mountains. The structure is a perfect fusion of traditional materials on the inside with an uncompromising contemporary protective shell. On the back of the pavilion the exposed wood is treated with pine tar, a sticky, sap-like material the result of the decomposition of pine through the application of excessive heat. Once the pine is broken down, pine tar is the result, used in shipbuilding for hundreds of years to seal the hulls of sailing vessels.

A gathering place in the best traditions of the Norwegian mountain hut, the pavilion was commissioned by the Norwegian Wild Reindeer Foundation to provide visitors with a view over the reindeer's terrain. Snøhetta's design echoes other architectural projects of the Norwegian National Tourist Routes Project, a series of viewing platforms and installations found along western Norway's 18 Designated Scenic Routes.

When the Norwegian constitution was finalized in 1814 the delegates chose the mountains of Dovrefjell to symbolize the strength of the independent, democratic nation they had forged. 'Agreed and faithful till Dovre falls', was the cry. Dovrefjell is also a place of myth and legend. It is here that a race of Norwegian giants took into their care Harald I, the son of Norway's first king prior to his return to Oslo to claim the throne. So there's no shortage of things to ponder as you settle down into Snøhetta's sculpted refuge, and await the arrival of Dovrefjell's wandering herds.

First published in 2019 by New Holland Publishers
London • Sydney • Auckland

Bentinck House, 3–8 Bolsover Street, London W1W 6AB, UK
1/66 Gibbes Street, Chatswood, NSW 2067, Australia
5/39 Woodside Ave, Northcote, Auckland 0627, New Zealand

newhollandpublishers.com

A record of this book is held at the British Library and the National Library of Australia.

ISBN 9781760790035

Group Managing Director: Fiona Schultz
Publisher: Alan Whiticker
Project Editor: Elise James
Designer: Andrew Davies
Production Director: Arlene Gippert
Printer: Toppan Leefung Printing Limited

10 9 8 7 6 5 4 3 2 1

Keep up with New Holland Publishers:
facebook.com/NewHollandPublishers
@newhollandpublishers

Picture Credits

In order of appearance: COVER © Hufton+Crow / Adam Mork • Page 1 © Henrik Kam • Page 2–3 © Martin Jochman • Page 4–5 © Aman Resorts • Pages 6, 8, 9 © Renzo Piano Building Workshop / Enrico Cano / Ruben Bescos • MORPHEUS HOTEL © City of Dreams • AMANGIRI © Aman Resorts • FORO BOCA © Jaime Navarro and Paul Rivera • QATAR NATIONAL LIBRARY © Qatar National Library • SHIMAO WONDERLAND INTERCONTINENTAL HOTEL © Martin Jochman • CITADEL UNIVERSITY CAMPUS © Renzo Piano Building Workshop • LA VALLETTA CITY GATE © Renzo Piano Building Workshop / Michel Denance • CENTRO BOTIN © Renzo Piano Building Workshop / Enrico Cano / Ruben Bescos • HARBIN OPERA HOUSE © Hufton+Crow / Adam Mork • VOXMAN MUSIC BUILDING © LMN Architects and Tim Griffith • NANJING ZENDAI HIMALAYAS CENTRE © CreatAR Images • CHAOYANG PARK PLAZA © Hufton+Crow • V&A DUNDEE-Hufton+Crow • TIRPITZ MUSEUM © BIG / Rasmus Hjortshoj / Laurian Ghinitoiu • SAN FRANCISCO MUSEUM OF MODERN ART © Henrik Kam • ZHANG ZHIDONG & MODERN INDUSTRIAL MUSEUM © Hufton+Crow • 007 ELEMENTS © Kristopher Grunert / David Schreyer / Jason O'Rear • FONDATION LOUIS VUITTON © Iwan Batiment / Todd Eberle • NIKE BOX MSK © Yuri Palmin • KOLON ONE & ONLY © Morphosis Architects / Jasmine Park • LEGO HOUSE © Iwan Baan • VIA 57 WEST © Iwan Baan • TINY TOWER © Sam Oberter • FREEBOOTER © Francisco Nogueira / Juliana Gomez / Michael Sieber • THE 7th ROOM © Peter Lundstrom / John Butlin • BRICK CAVE © Nguyen Tien Thanh • DON JUAN HOUSE © Jag Studio • PATIO HOUSE © Yorgos Kordakis • KLEIN A45 © Matthew Carbone • THE SKYWALK © Stephen Ball • TUNNEL OF LIGHT © Echigo Tsumari • NORWEGIAN WILD REINDEER PAVILION © Ketil Jacobsen

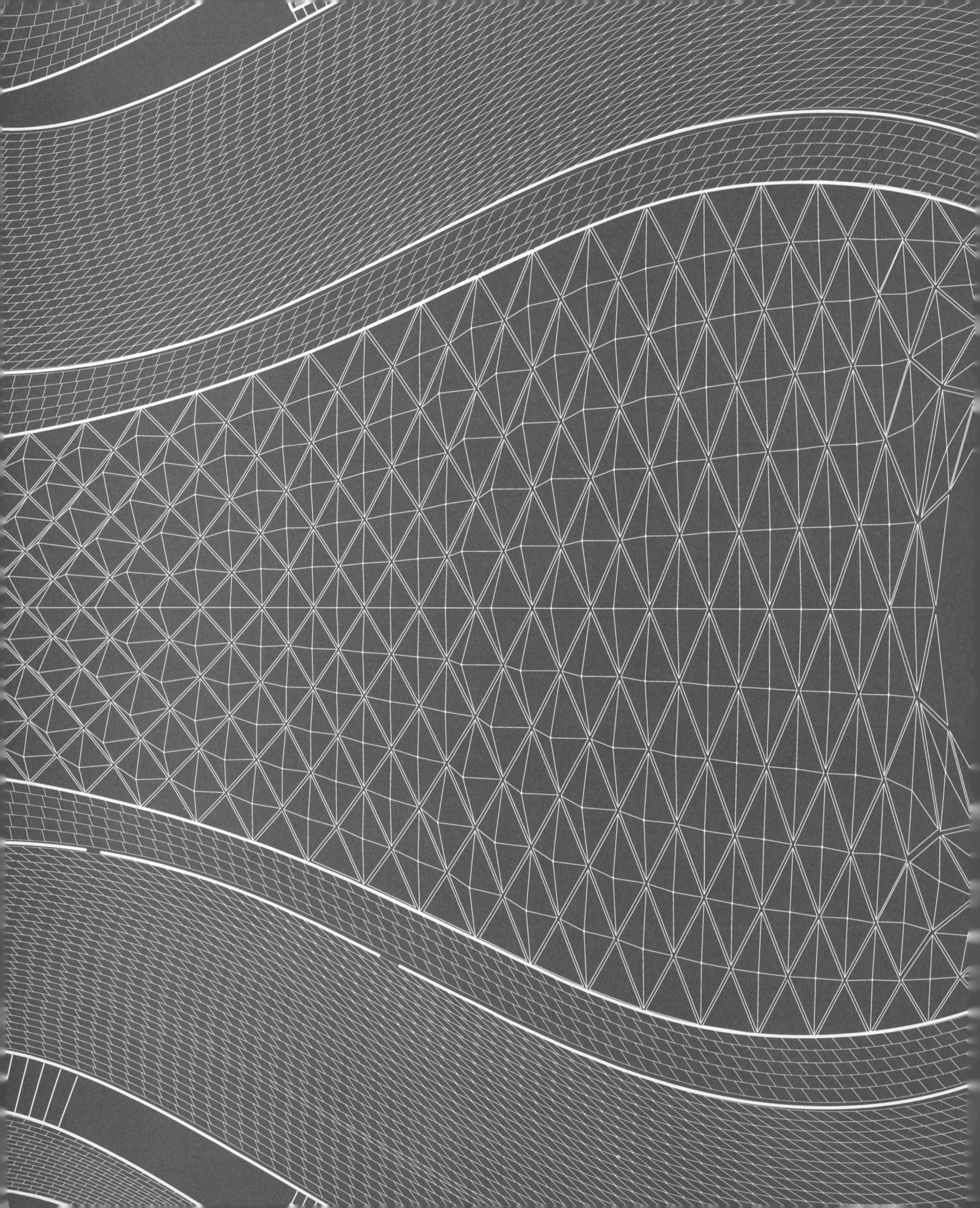